Easy Piano
Vocal Selections

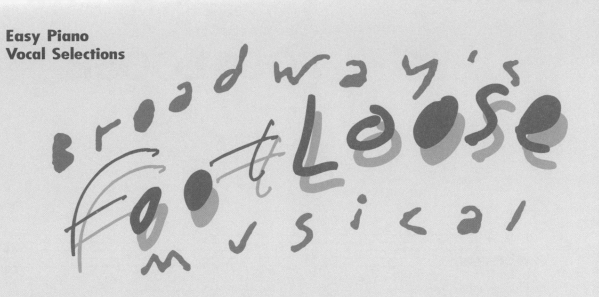

Broadway's Footloose Musical

ISBN 978-1-4584-2013-8

HAL•LEONARD®
CORPORATION

7777 W. BLUEMOUND RD. P.O. BOX 13819 MILWAUKEE, WI 53213

In Australia contact:
Hal Leonard Australia Pty. Ltd.
4 Lentara Court
Cheltenham, Victoria, 3192 Australia
Email: ausadmin@halleonard.com.au

Visit Hal Leonard Online at
www.halleonard.com

FOOTLOOSE

Words by DEAN PITCHFORD
Music by KENNY LOGGINS

I been work - in' so hard.
You're play - in' so cool,

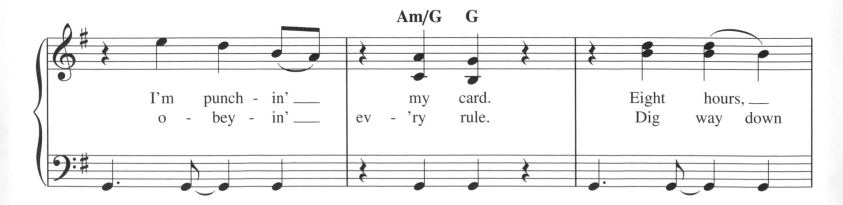

I'm punch - in' my card.
o - bey - in' ev - 'ry rule.

Eight hours,
Dig way down

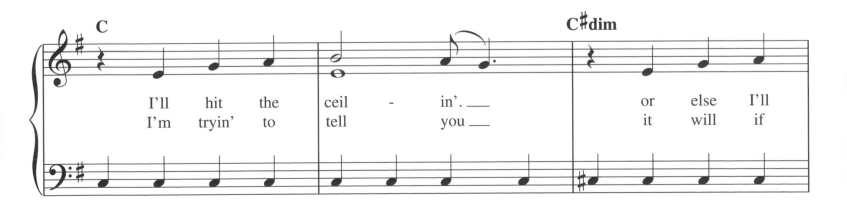

4

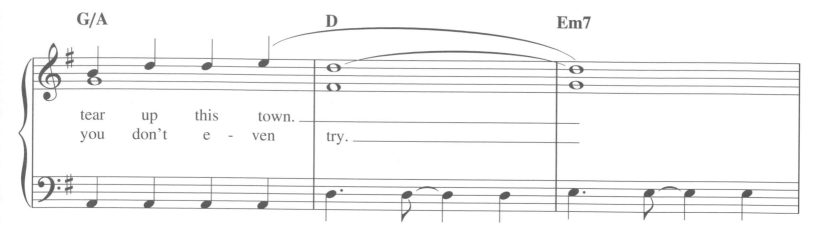

tear up this town.
you don't e - ven try.

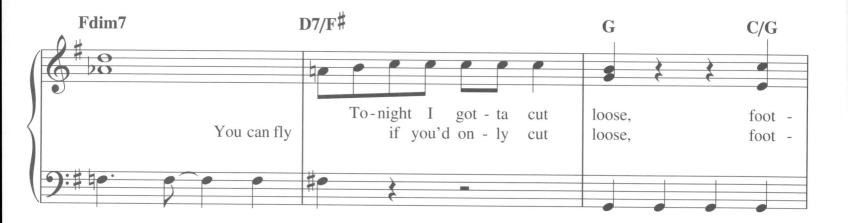

You can fly
To - night I got - ta cut loose, foot -
if you'd on - ly cut loose, foot -

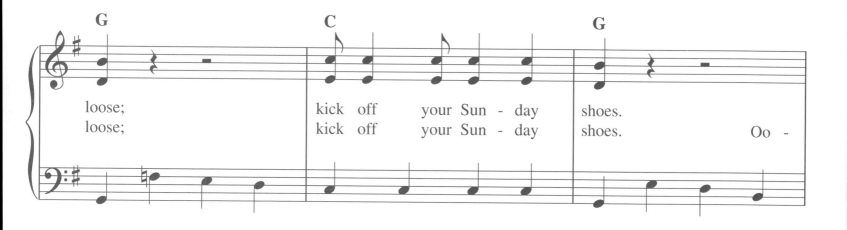

loose; kick off your Sun - day shoes.
loose; kick off your Sun - day shoes. Oo -

Please, Lou - ise, pull me off ___ of my
ee, Ma - rie, shake it, shake _ it for

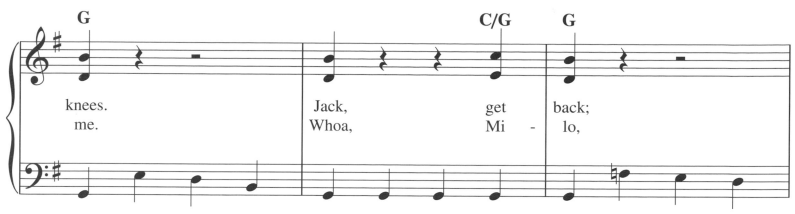

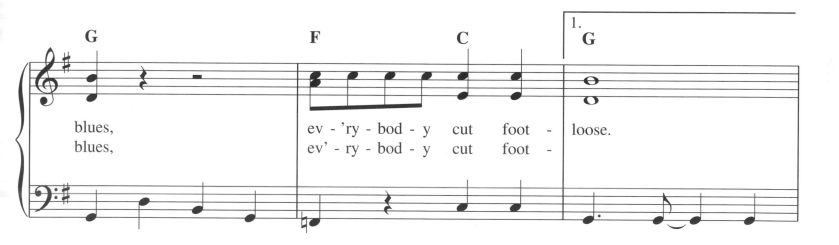

THE GIRL GETS AROUND

Words by DEAN PITCHFORD
Music by SAMMY HAGAR

Driving Rock 'n' Roll

But I've seen how she moves and this girl

real - ly cooks. She taught me some tricks you can't

learn in books, and I'm start - ing to think she's the

dev - il in dis - guise.

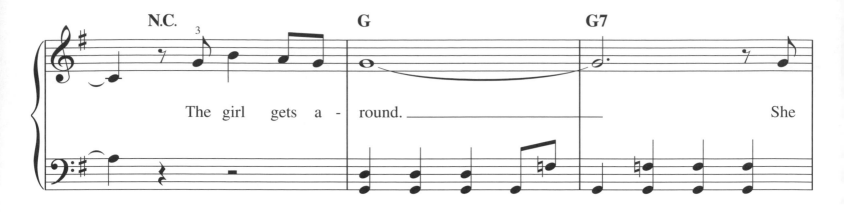

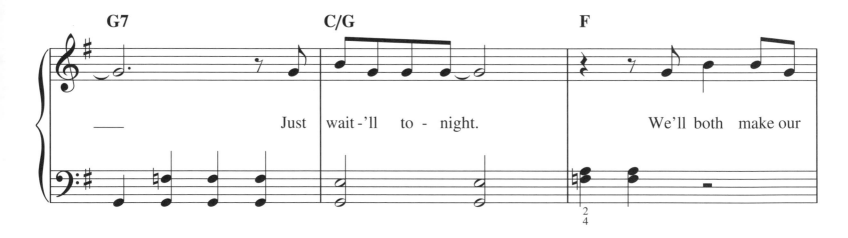

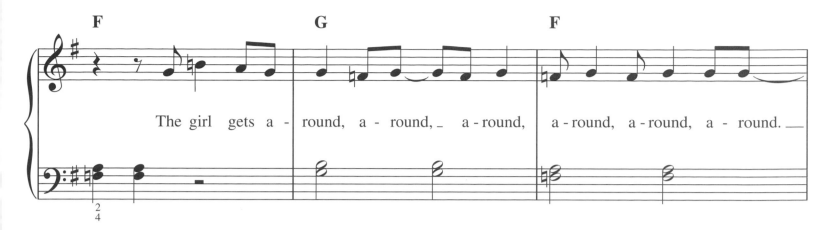

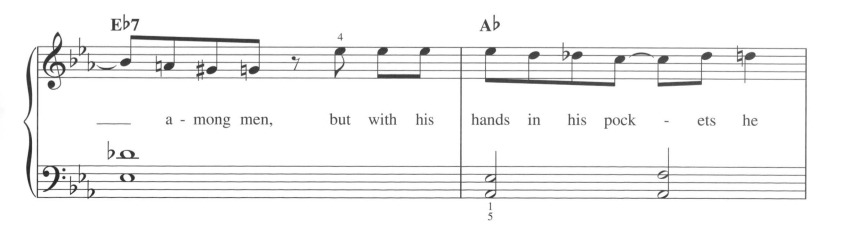

can't count to ten. ___ Don't wor - ry, ba - by, your

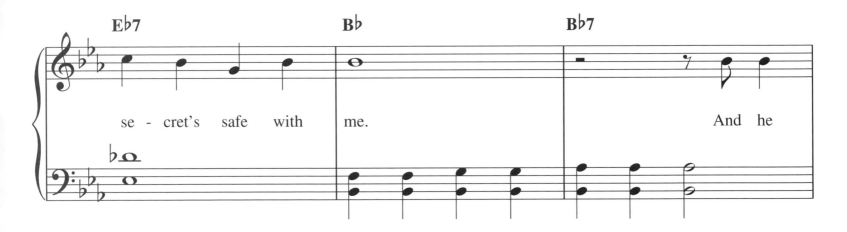

se - cret's safe with me. And he

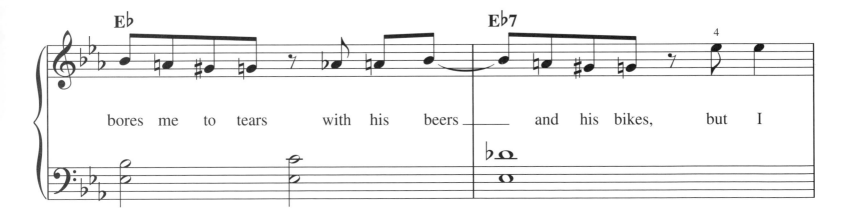

bores me to tears with his beers ___ and his bikes, but I

keep him a - round ___ 'cause when temp - ta - tion strikes,

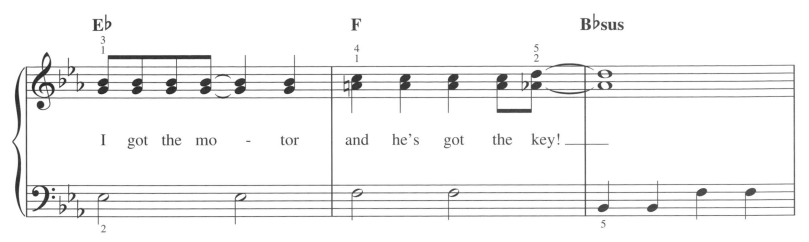

I got the mo - tor and he's got the key!

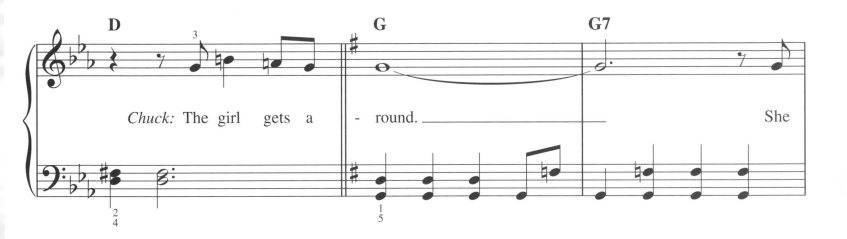

Chuck: The girl gets a - round. ____ She

knows what she likes. I've got what she needs. ____

Just wait-'ll to - night. _ *Both:* We'll both make our

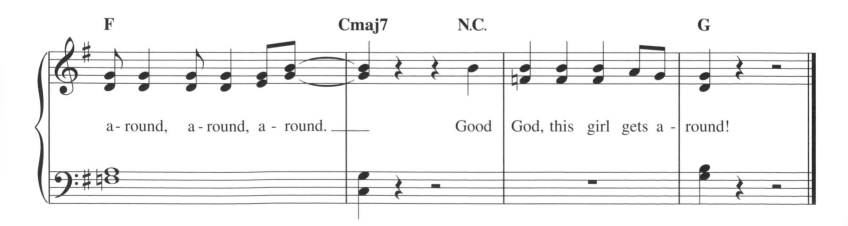

HOLDING OUT FOR A HERO

Words by DEAN PITCHFORD
Music by JIM STEINMAN

Slowly, freely

mf Where have all the good men gone, and where are all the gods? _

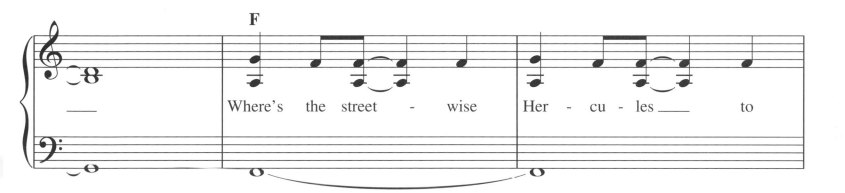

_ Where's the street - wise Her - cu - les _ to

fight the ris - ing odds? _ Is - n't there a white _ knight up

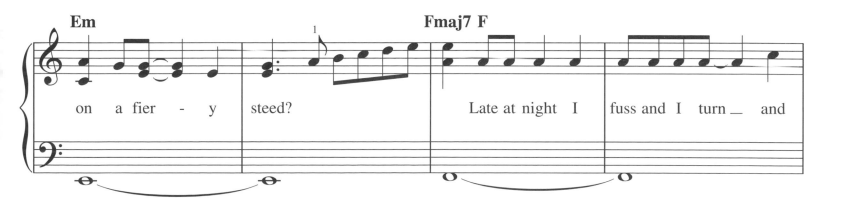

on a fier - y steed? Late at night I fuss and I turn _ and

Disco Appassionato

dream of what I need._____ I need a he - ro.

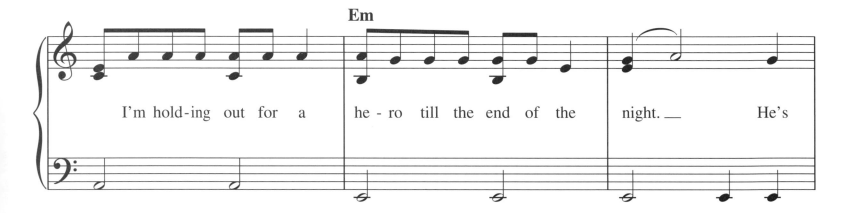

I'm hold-ing out for a he - ro till the end of the night.__ He's

got - ta be strong _ and he's got - ta be fast __ and he's got - ta be fresh _ from the

fight. I need a he - ro. I'm hold-ing out for a

he - ro till the morn - ing ___ light. ___ He's got - ta be sure ___ and it's

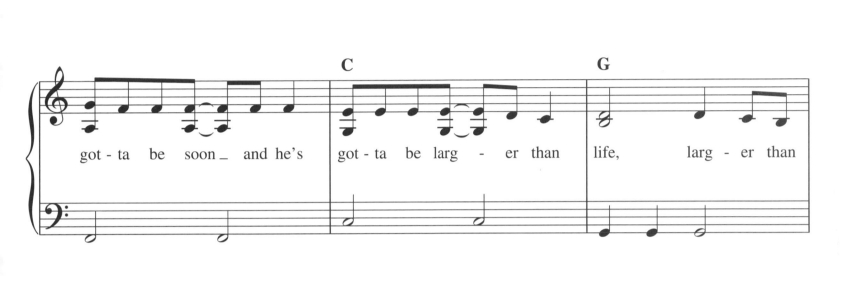

got - ta be soon ___ and he's got - ta be larg - er than life, larg - er than

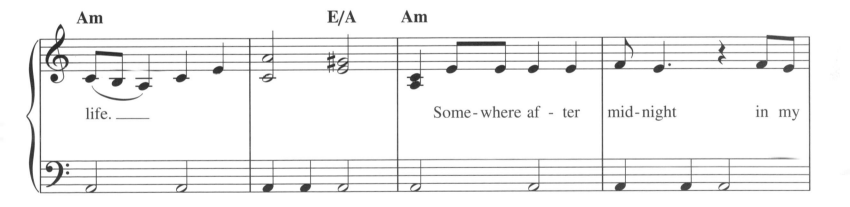

life. ___ Some - where af - ter mid - night in my

wild - est fan - ta - sy, some - where just ___ be -

yond my reach, __ there's some - one reach - ing back for me.

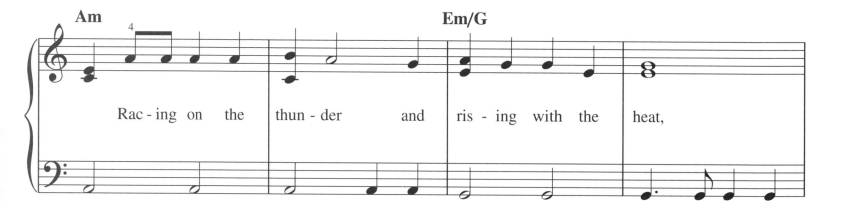

Rac - ing on the thun - der and ris - ing with the heat,

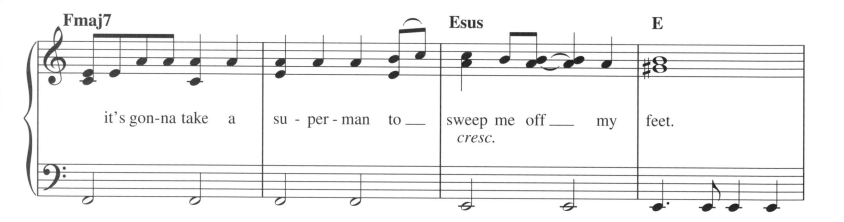

it's gon-na take a su - per - man to __ sweep me off __ my feet.

cresc.

Up where the moun-tains meet the heav-ens a - bove, _____

out where the light-ning splits the sea, _____ I could swear _ there is

some-one some-where watch-ing _ me. _

Through the wind and the chill and the rain _ and the storm _ and the

flood, _____ I can feel _ this ap - proach like a fire _ in my

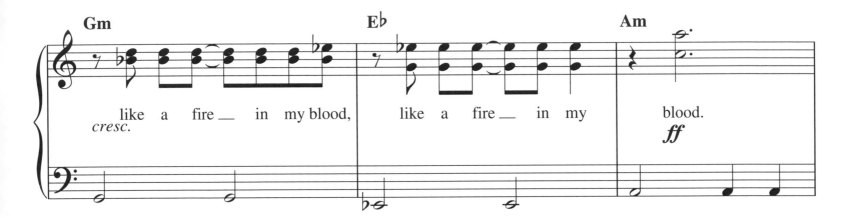

F **Fm** **Db/F** **Fm**

blood, ___ like a fire ___ in my blood, like a fire ___ in my blood,

Gm **Eb** **Am**

like a fire ___ in my blood, like a fire ___ in my blood.

cresc. *ff*

E **Am**

Ah! ___ I need a he - ro. I'm hold-ing out for a

Em **F**

he - ro till the morn - ing ___ light. ___ And he's got-ta be sure ___ and it's

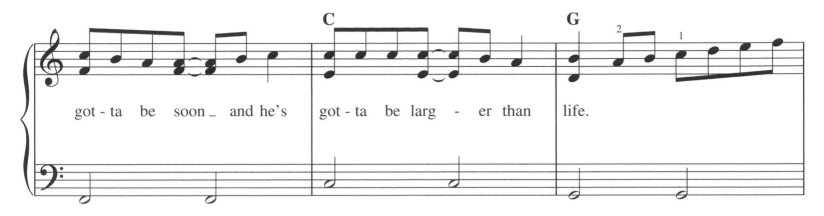

got - ta be soon _ and he's got - ta be larg – er than life.

Oh, he's

got - ta be strong _ and he's got - ta be fast _ and he's got - ta be fresh _ from the

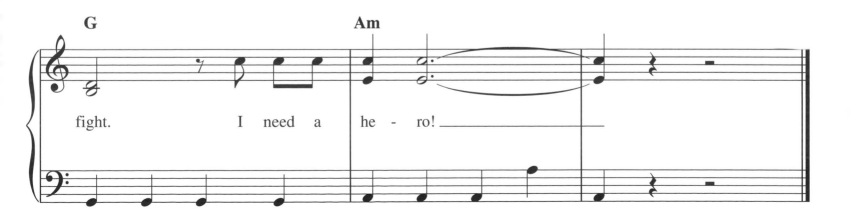

fight. I need a he - ro! _____

I CAN'T STAND STILL

Words by DEAN PITCHFORD
Music by TOM SNOW

Moving along, in 2

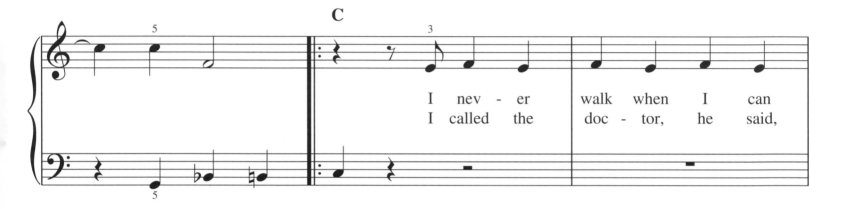

I nev - er walk when I can
I called the doc - tor, he said,

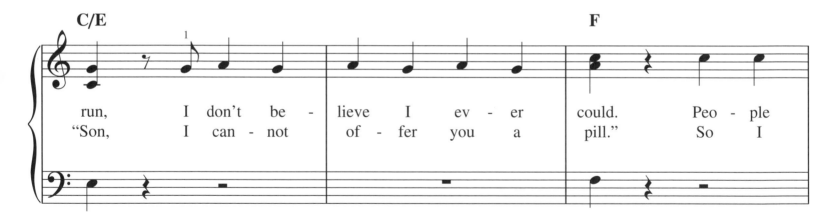

run, I don't be - lieve I ev - er could. Peo - ple
"Son, I can - not of - fer you a pill." So I

try to slow ___ me down, say - ing "Boy, you real - ly
nev - er found ___ re - lief and now I've got to move ___ un -

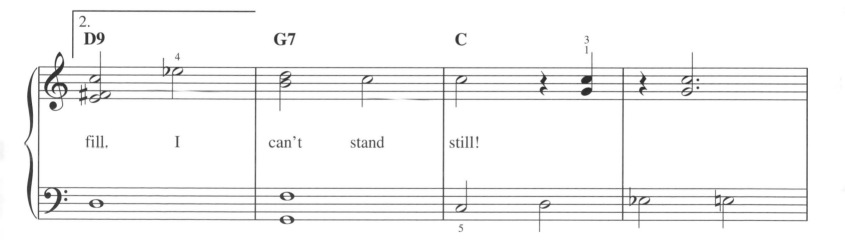

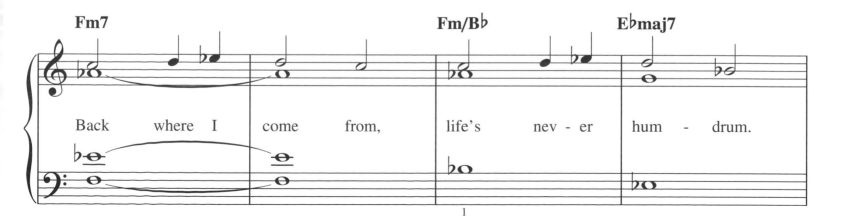

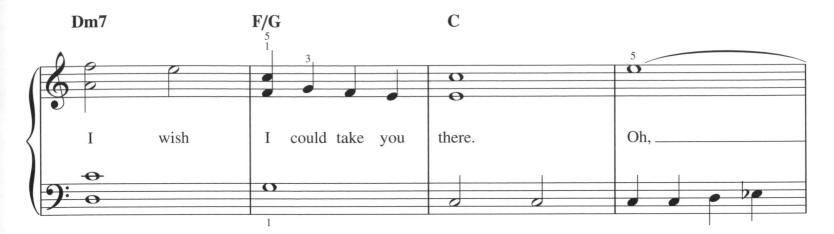

I wish I could take you there. Oh, _____

_____ we had the world at our

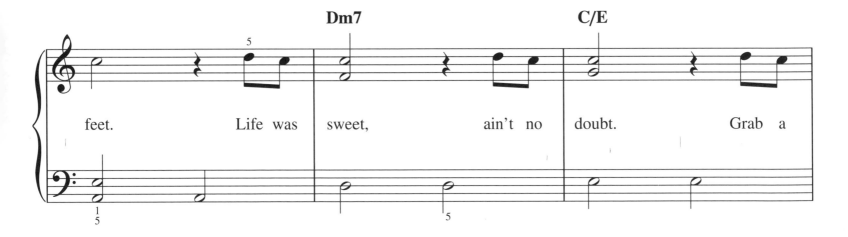

feet. Life was sweet, ain't no doubt. Grab a

seat, check it out.

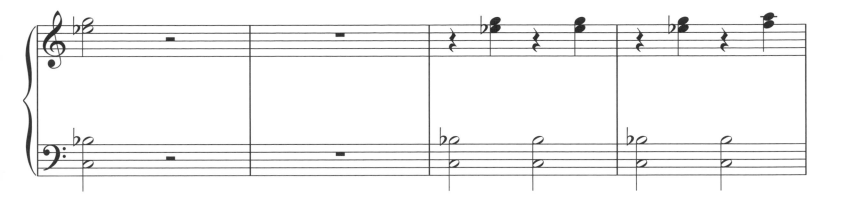

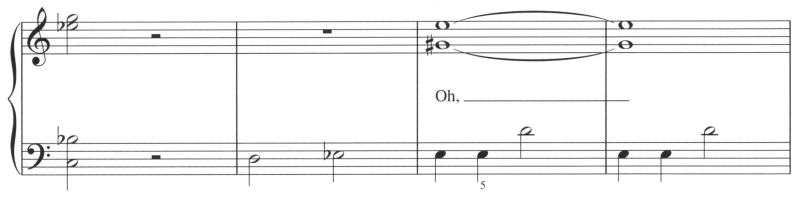

Oh, _____

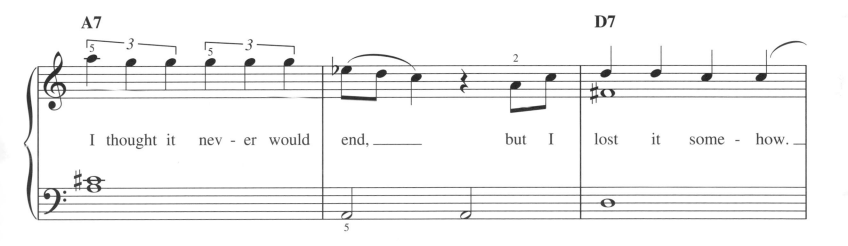

I thought it nev - er would end, ____ but I lost it some - how. __

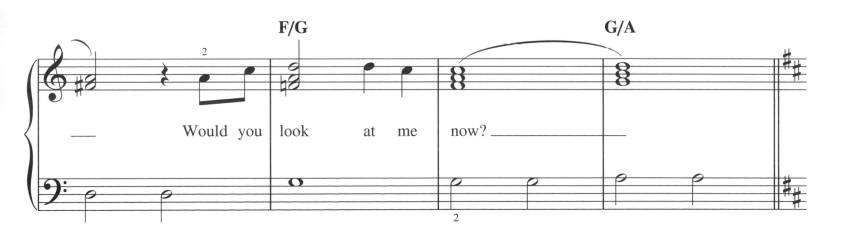

__ Would you look at me now? _____

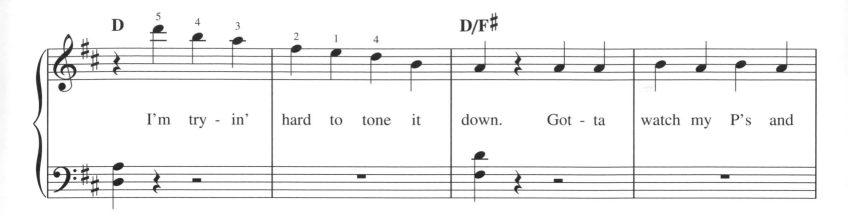

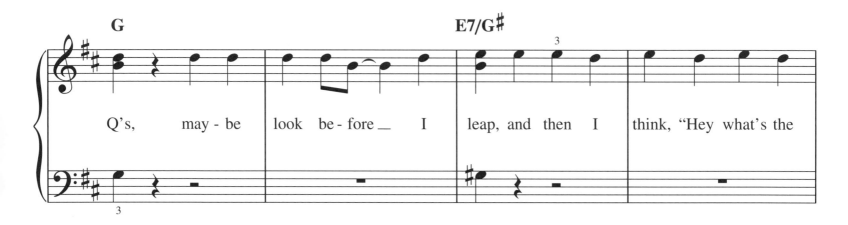

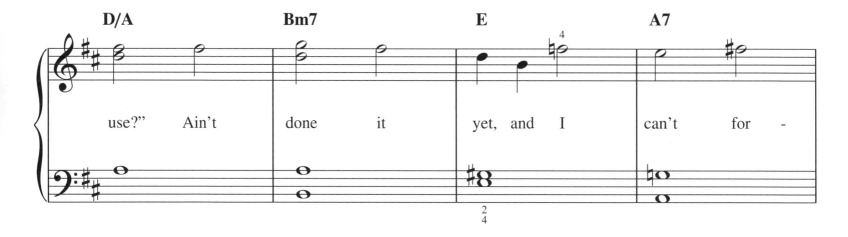

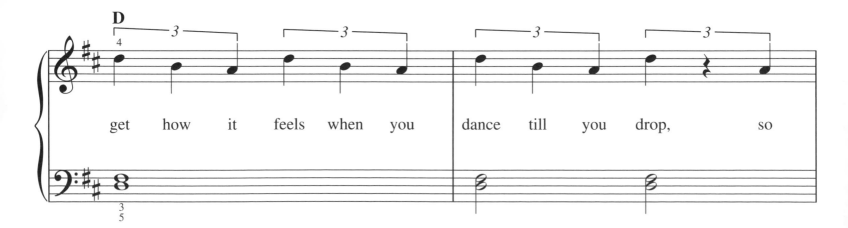

don't e - ven start to sug - gest that I stop.

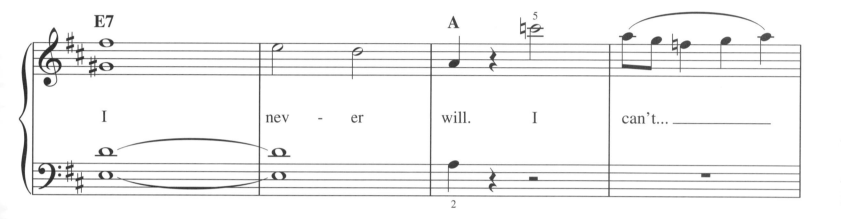

I nev - er will. I can't...

No, no, no, no. I can't stand

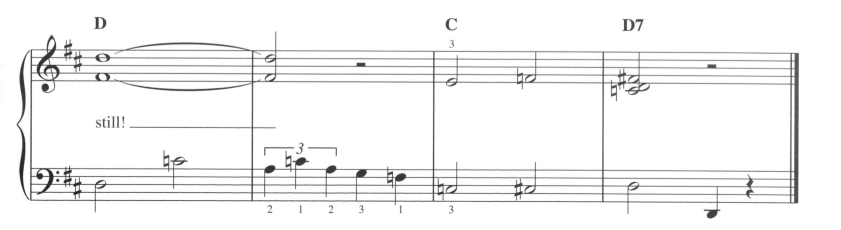

still!

SOMEBODY'S EYES

Words by DEAN PITCHFORD
Music by TOM SNOW

Tense and precise

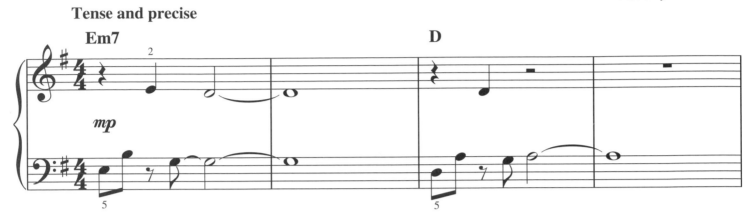

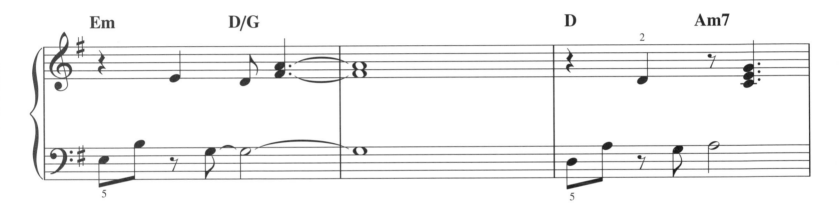

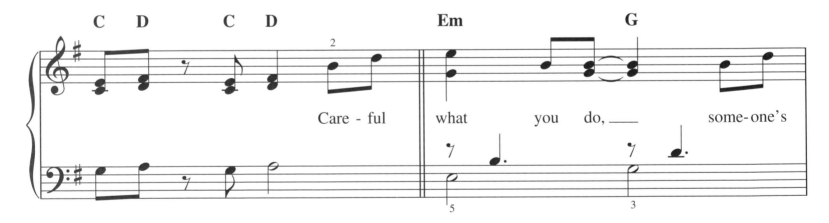

Care - ful   what   you   do, ___   some-one's

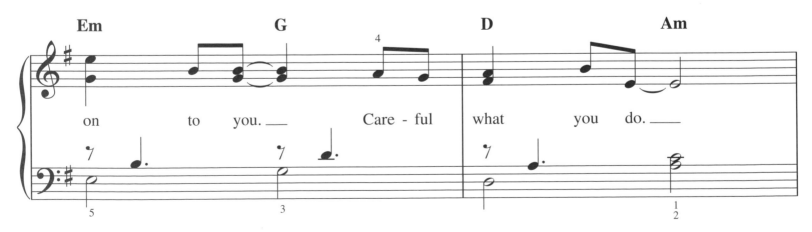

on   to   you. ___   Care - ful   what   you   do. ___

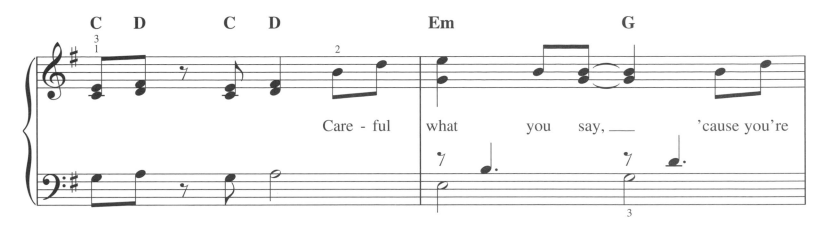

Care - ful what you say, ___ 'cause you're

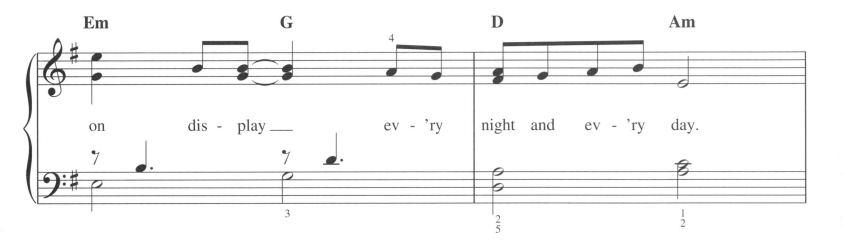

on dis - play ___ ev - 'ry night and ev - 'ry day.

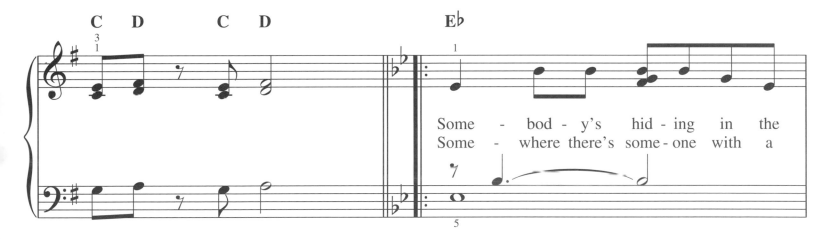

Some - bod - y's hid - ing in the
Some - where there's some - one with a

great un - known. ___ (Uh - huh.)
per - fect view. ___ (Yoo - hoo.)

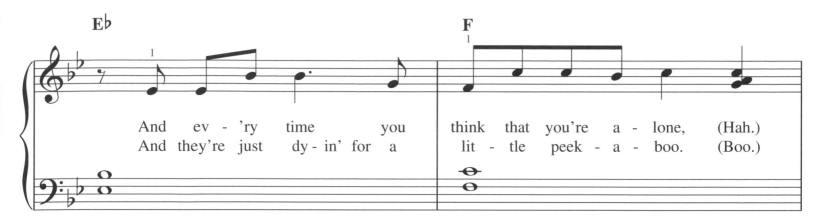

And ev - 'ry time you think that you're a - lone, (Hah.)
And they're just dy - in' for a lit - tle peek - a - boo. (Boo.)

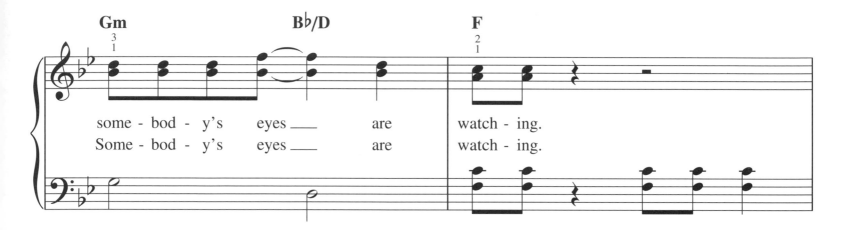

some - bod - y's eyes ___ are watch - ing.
Some - bod - y's eyes ___ are watch - ing.

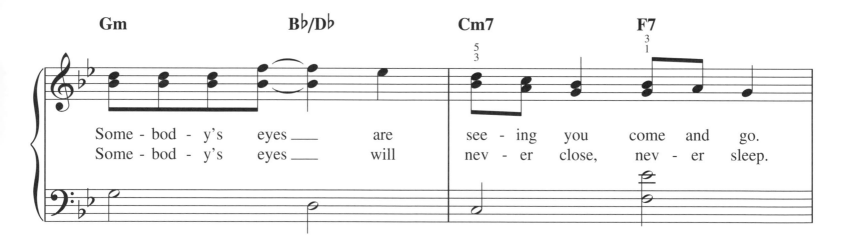

Some - bod - y's eyes ___ are see - ing you come and go.
Some - bod - y's eyes ___ will nev - er close, nev - er sleep.

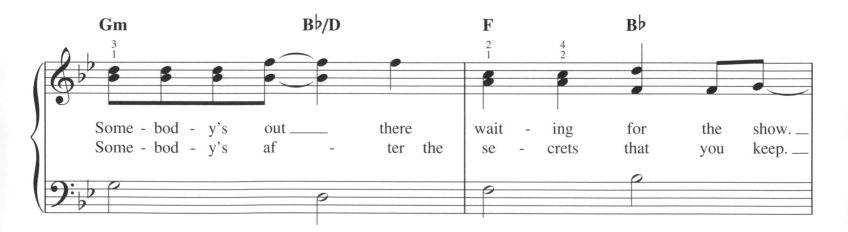

Some - bod - y's out ___ there wait - ing for the show. ___
Some - bod - y's af - ter the se - crets that you keep. ___

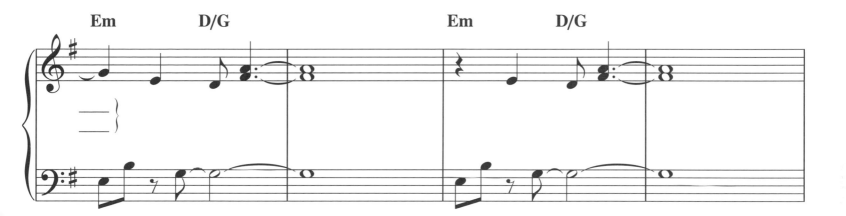

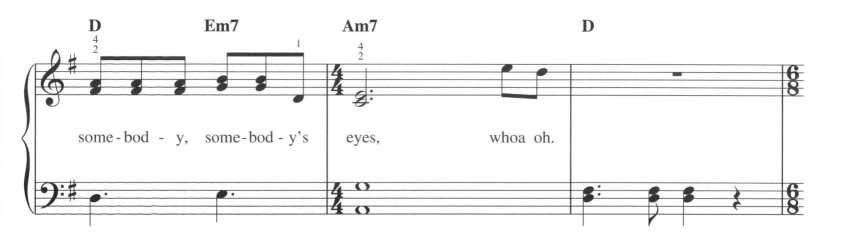

30

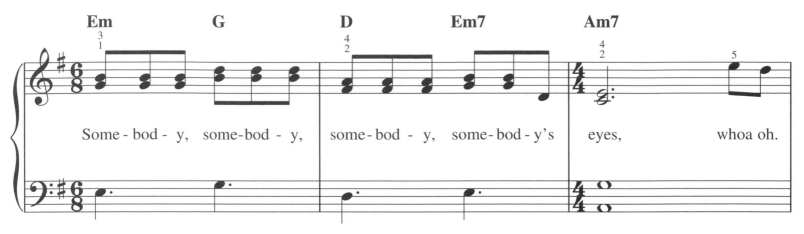

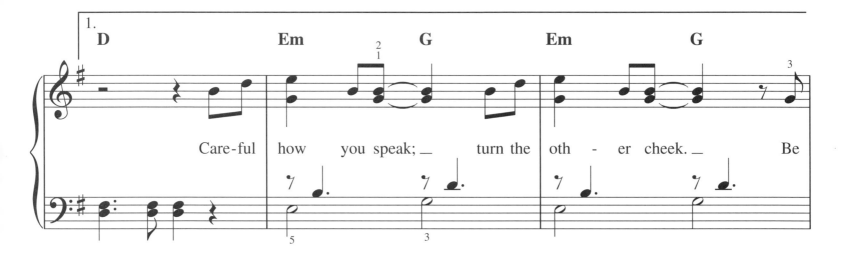

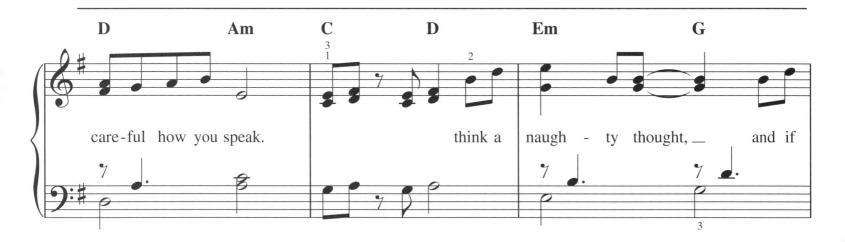

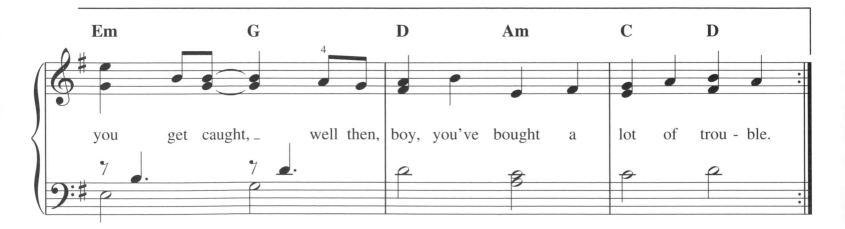

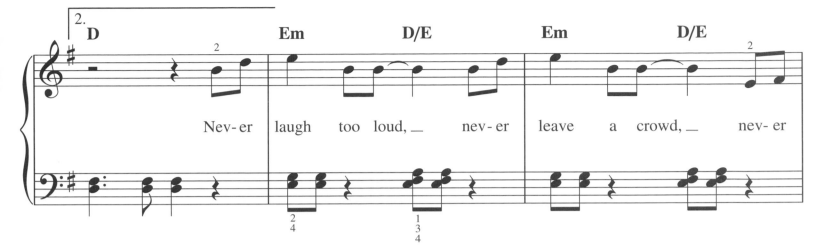

Nev-er laugh too loud, __ nev-er leave a crowd, __ nev-er

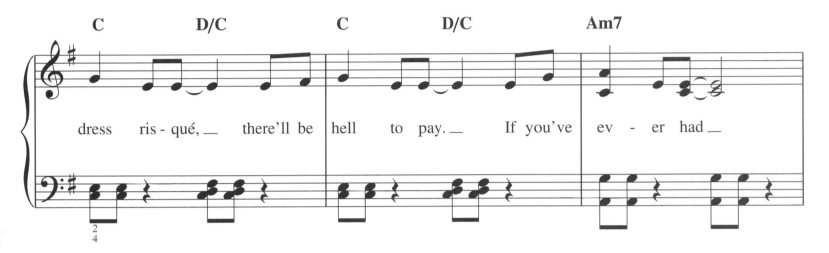

dress ris-qué, __ there'll be hell to pay. __ If you've ev-er had __

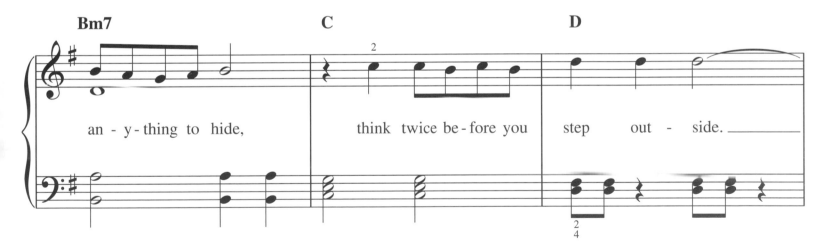

an-y-thing to hide, think twice be-fore you step out-side. __

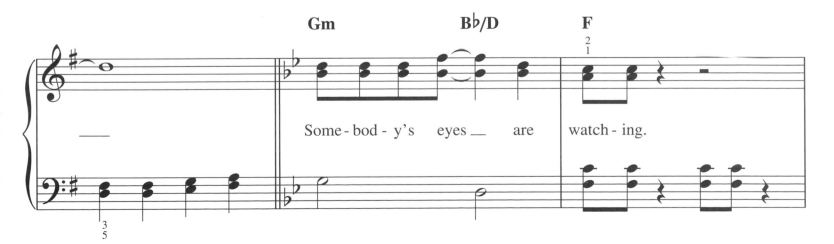

__ Some-bod-y's eyes __ are watch-ing.

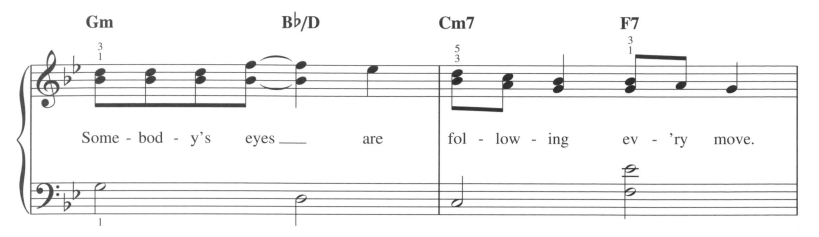

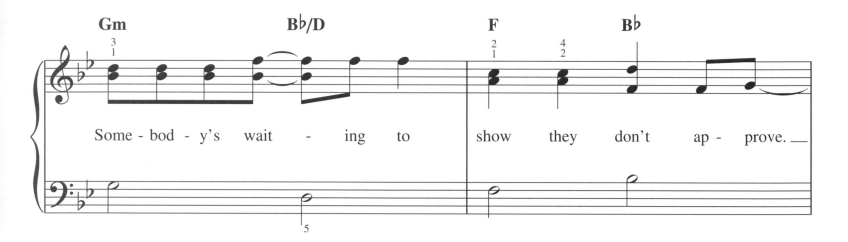

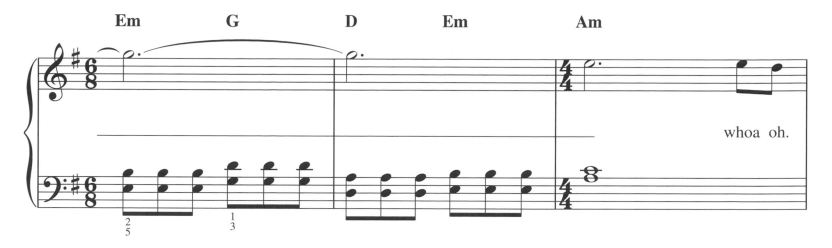

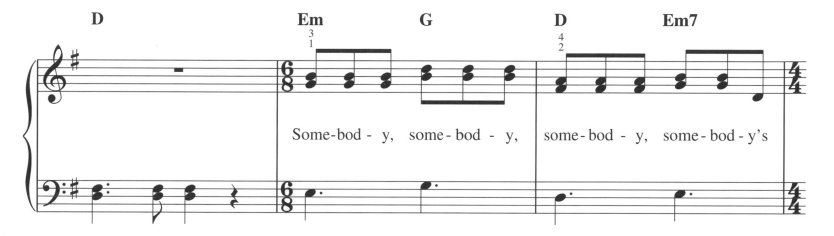

Some-bod - y, some-bod - y, some-bod - y, some-bod - y's

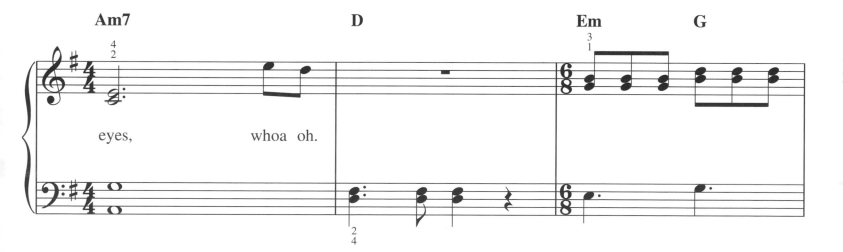

eyes, whoa oh.

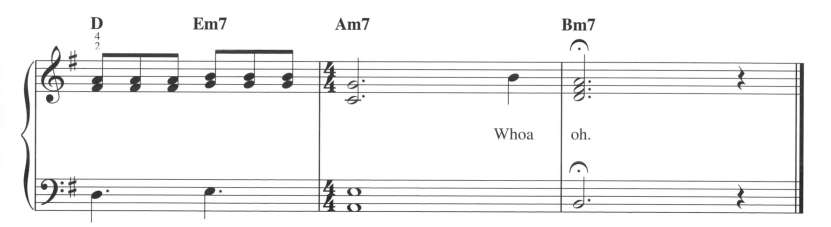

Whoa oh.

LEARNING TO BE SILENT

Words by DEAN PITCHFORD
Music by TOM SNOW

Flowing, in 2

Vi: Swal - low - ing my words, ___
Ethel: Watch - ing how the dust ___

star-ing at the floor, ___ count-ing lit - tle cracks in the
danc-es out the door, ___ no - tic - ing my hands start to

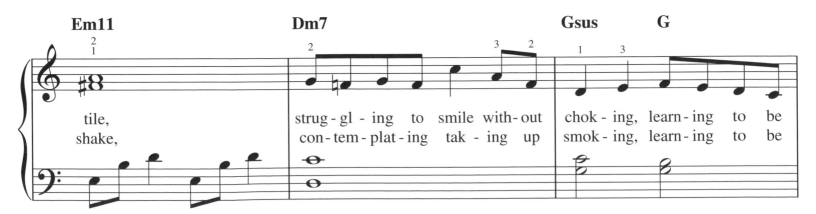

tile, strug - gl - ing to smile with-out chok - ing, learn - ing to be
shake, con - tem - plat - ing tak - ing up smok - ing, learn - ing to be

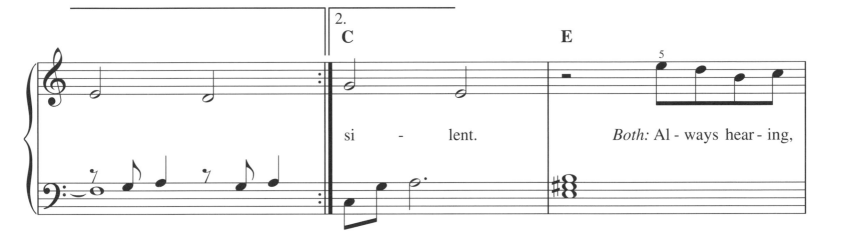

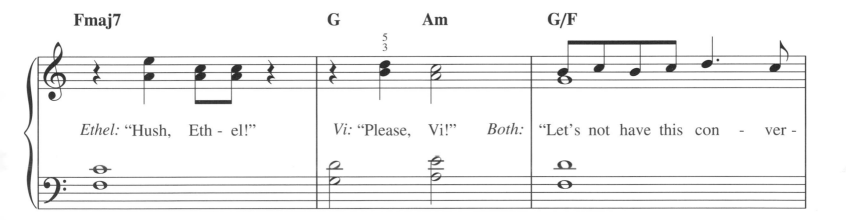

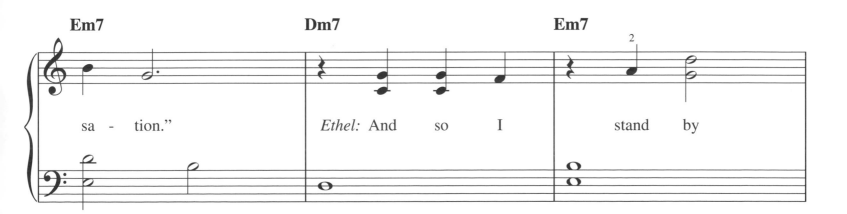

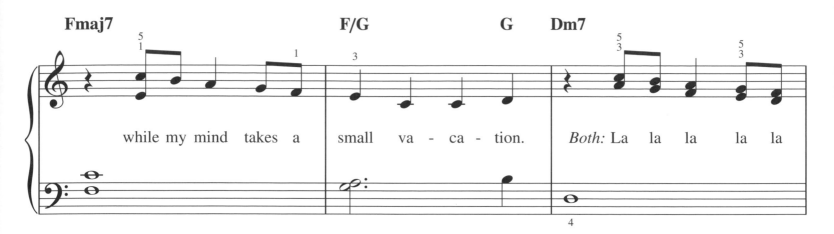

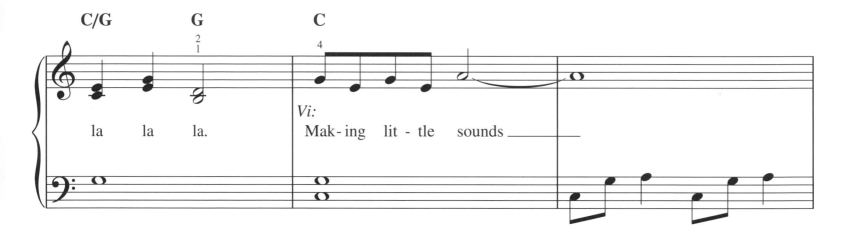

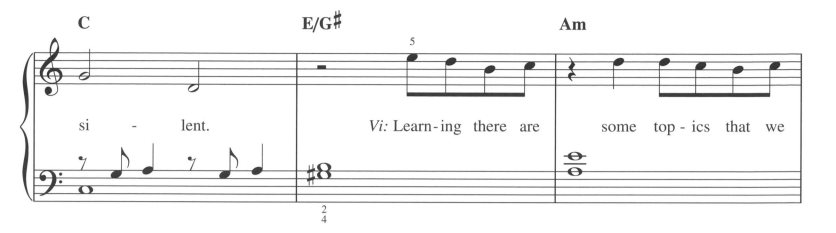

si - lent. *Vi:* Learn-ing there are some top - ics that we

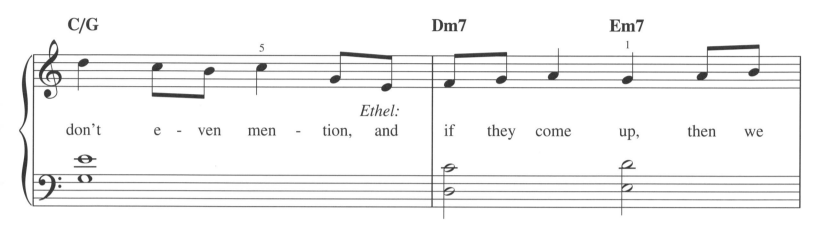

don't e - ven men - tion, and *Ethel:* if they come up, then we

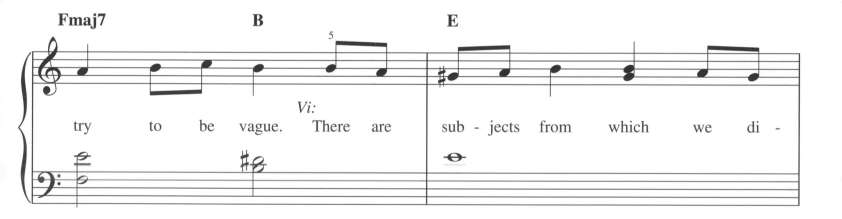

try to be vague. *Vi:* There are sub - jects from which we di -

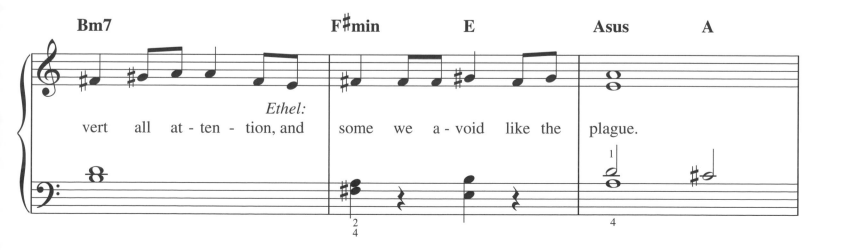

vert all at - ten - tion, and *Ethel:* some we a - void like the plague.

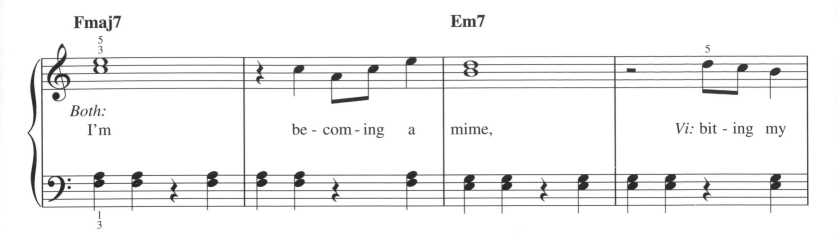

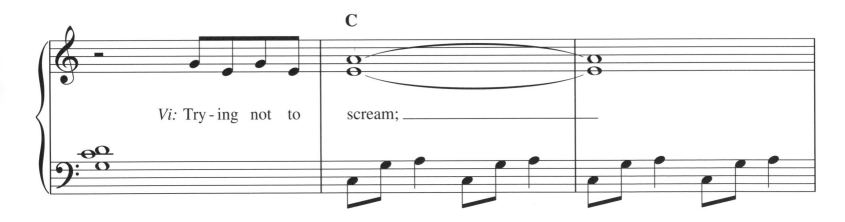

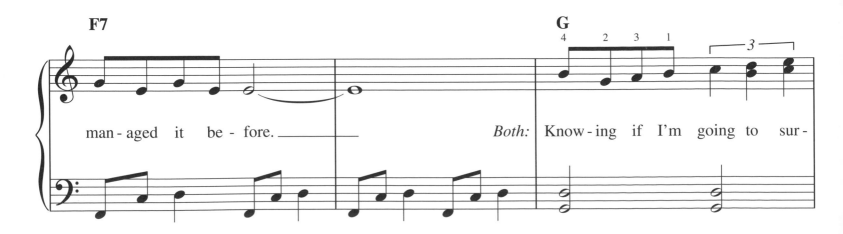

G#dim7   **Am**

vive,   then,   dam- mit,   *Ethel:* I've   got to

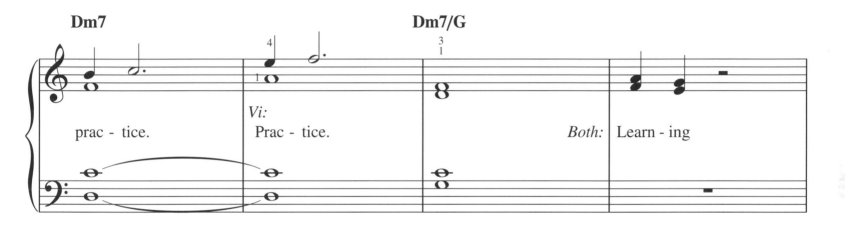

Dm7   **Dm7/G**

prac - tice.   *Vi:* Prac - tice.   *Both:* Learn - ing

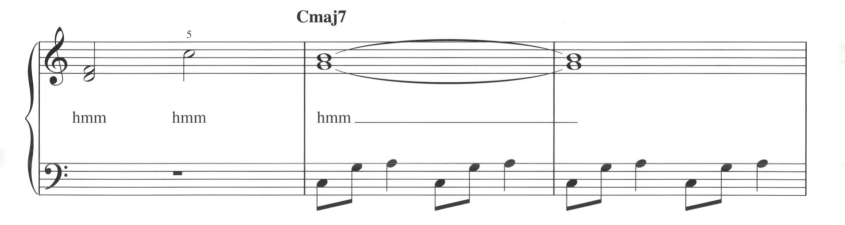

Cmaj7

hmm   hmm   hmm _____

Fmaj7   **C**

hmm. _____

HEAVEN HELP ME

Words by DEAN PITCHFORD
Music by TOM SNOW

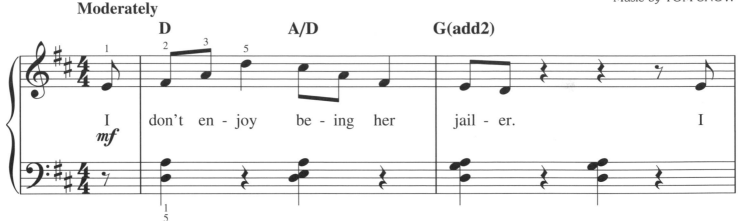

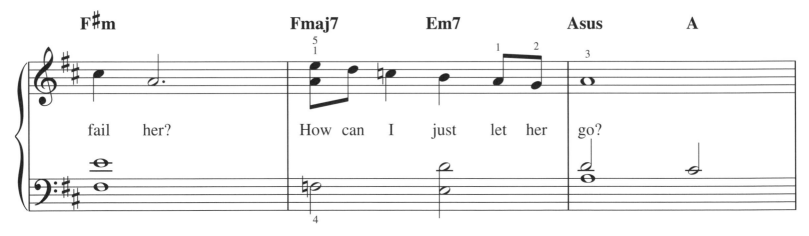

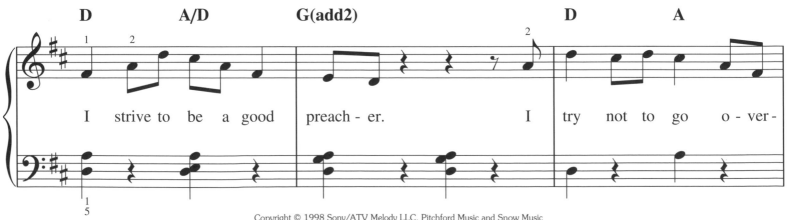

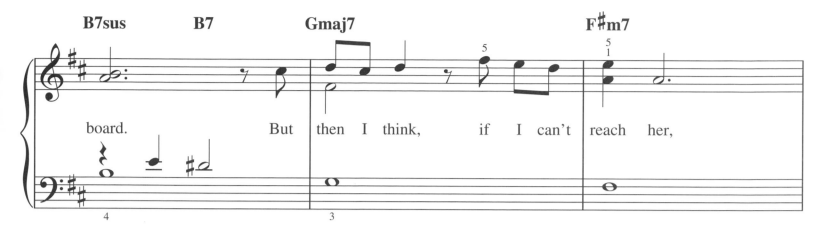

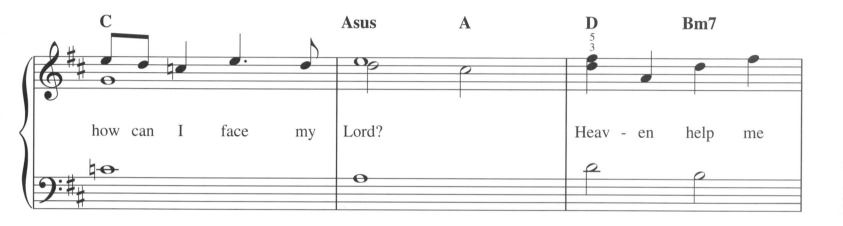

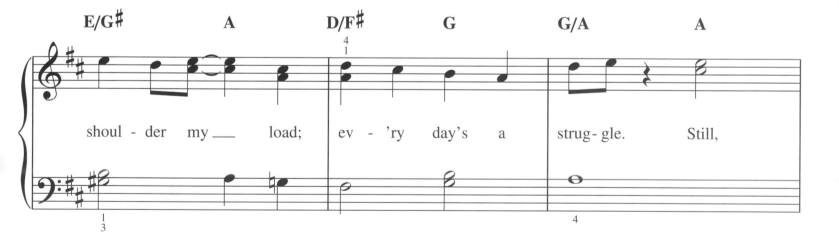

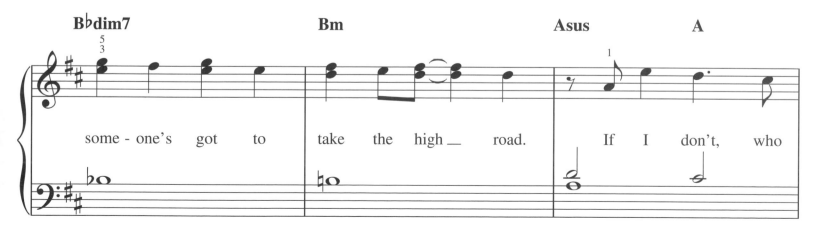

will? I be-came _ a man of God _

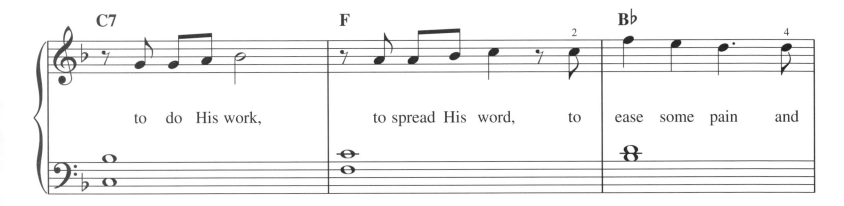

to do His work, to spread His word, to ease some pain and

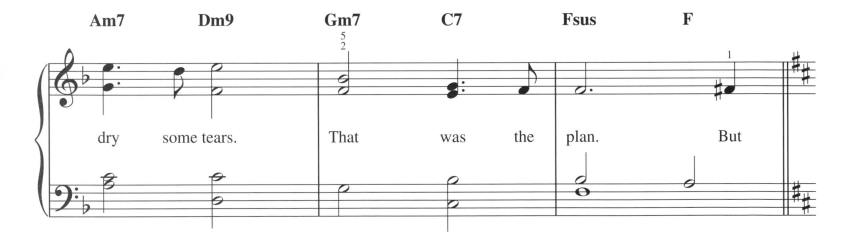

dry some tears. That was the plan. But

I might have thought twice

if on - ly I knew that

I'd spend all of my time say - ing,

"Ainh, ainh, ainh, no! No! Don't do that!"

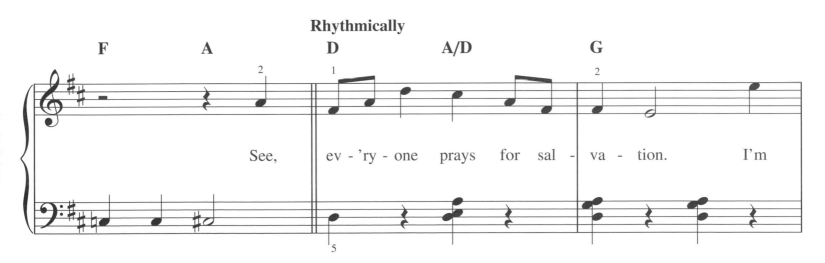

See, ev - 'ry - one prays for sal - va - tion. I'm

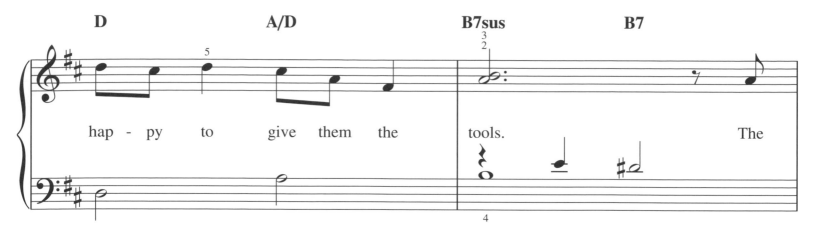

D **A/D** **B7sus** **B7**

hap - py to give them the tools. The

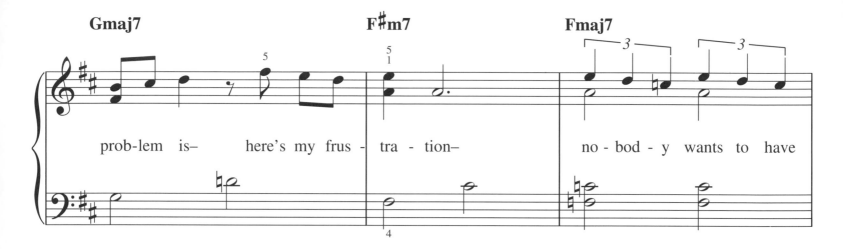

Gmaj7 **F♯m7** **Fmaj7**

prob-lem is– here's my frus - tra - tion– no - bod - y wants to have

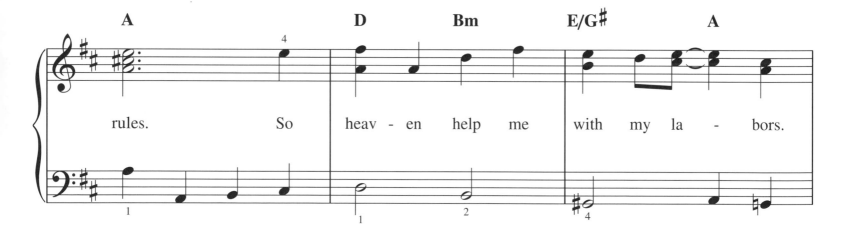

A **D** **Bm** **E/G♯** **A**

rules. So heav - en help me with my la - bors.

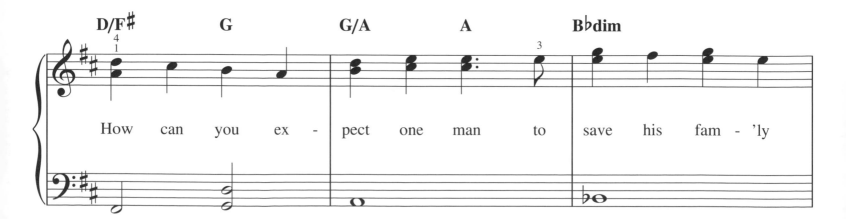

D/F♯ **G** **G/A** **A** **B♭dim**

How can you ex - pect one man to save his fam - 'ly

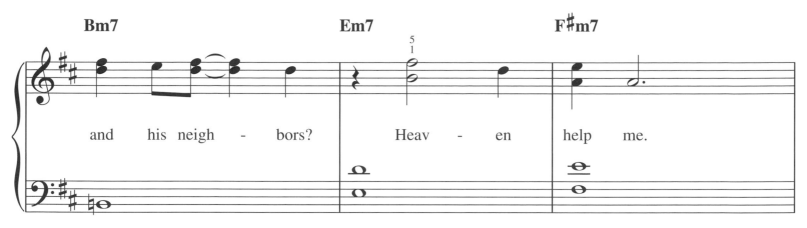

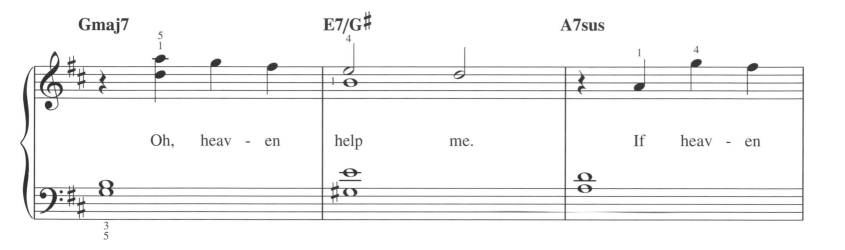

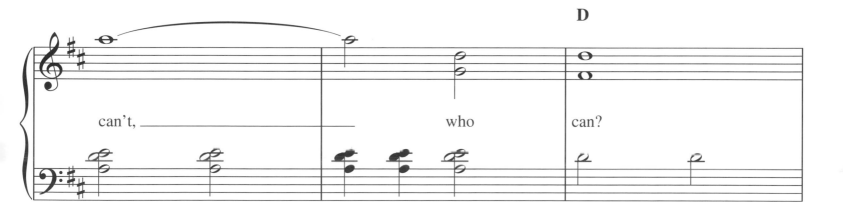

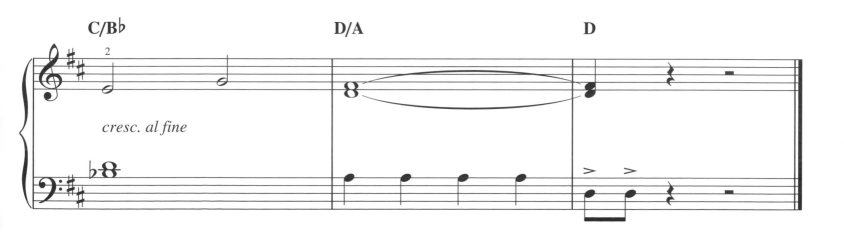

I'M FREE
(Heaven Helps the Man)

Words by DEAN PITCHFORD
Music by KENNY LOGGINS

Quickly, intense

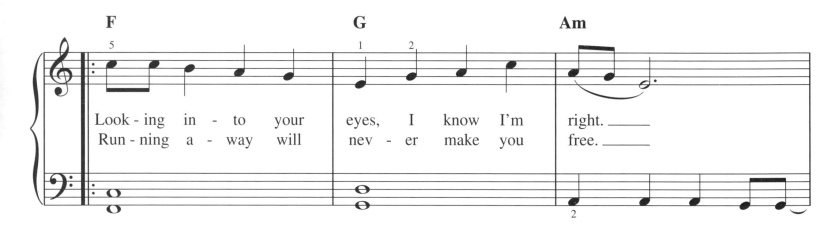

Look - ing in - to your eyes, I know I'm right. _____
Run - ning a - way will nev - er make you free. _____

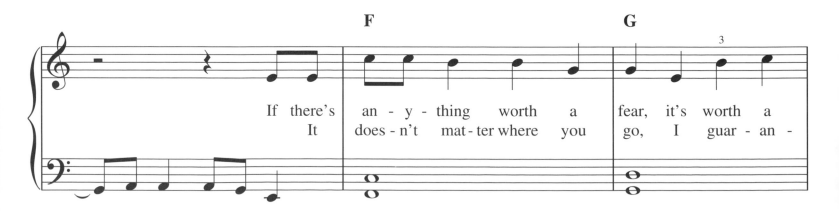

If there's an - y - thing worth a fear, it's worth a
It does - n't mat - ter where you go, I guar - an -

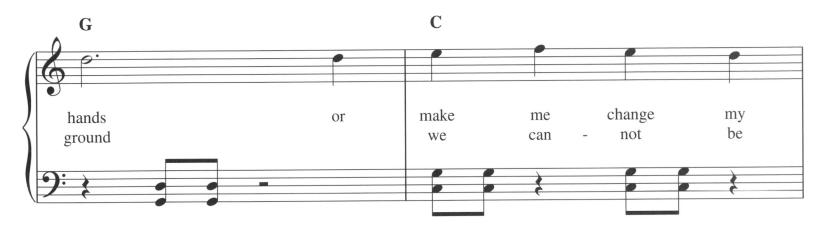

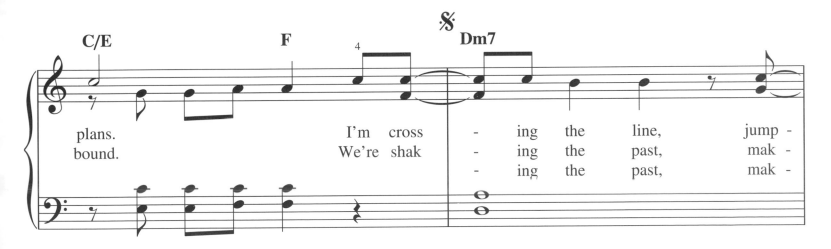

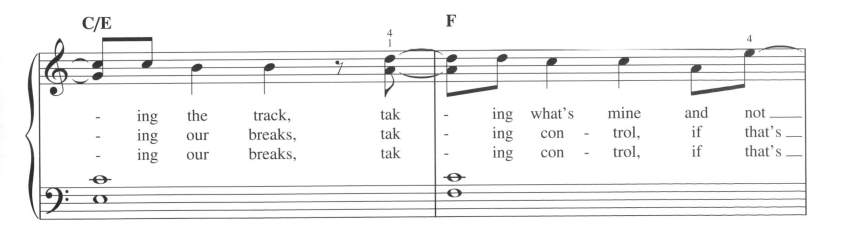

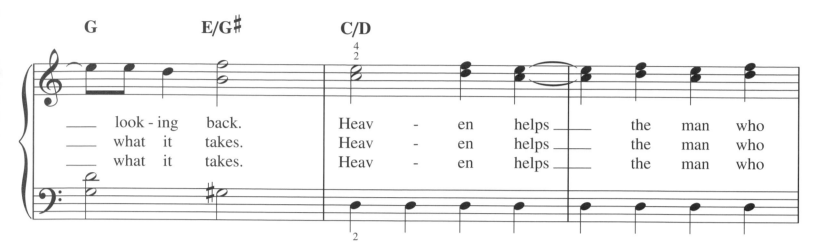

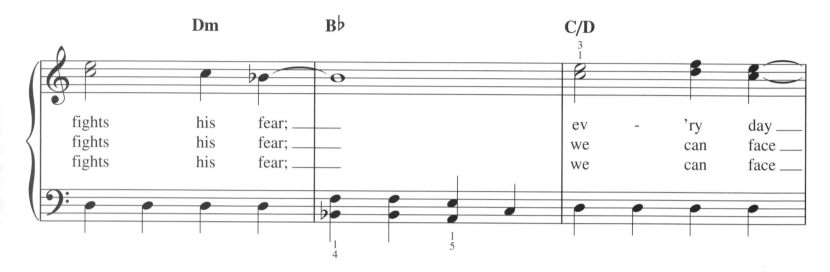

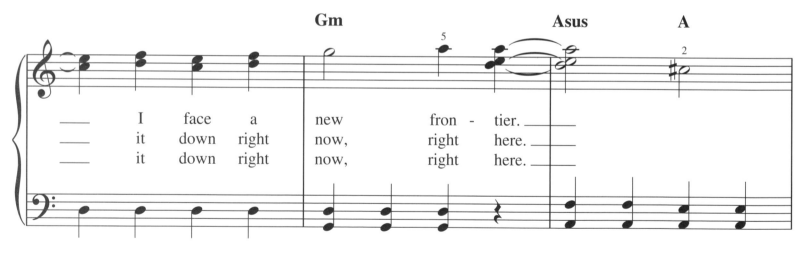

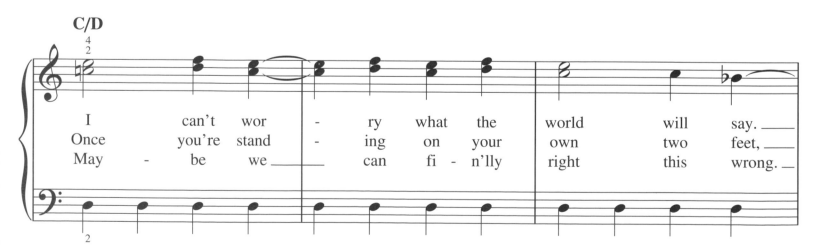

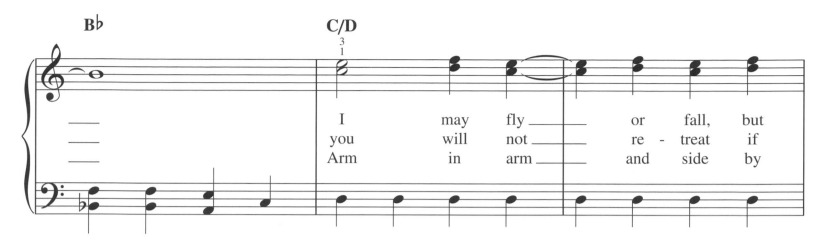

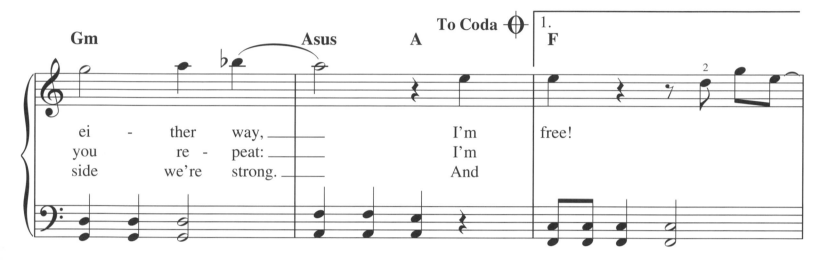

CODA **F** **G**

free!

G/A **Am** **Dm**

Heav - en helps ___ the man.

G/A **Dm** **E**

We can face ___ it down. Heav - en help me!

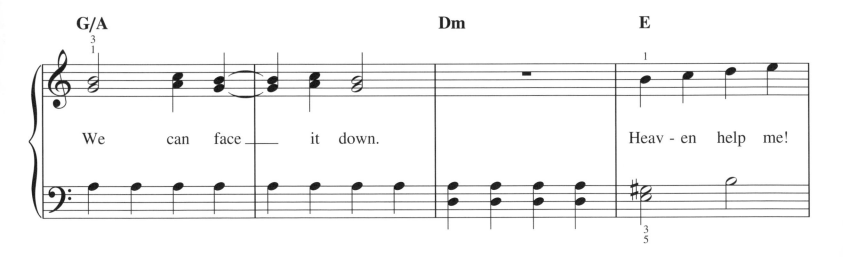

Dm **G7** **Cmaj7** **F**

Some - one's got to save his neigh - bors.

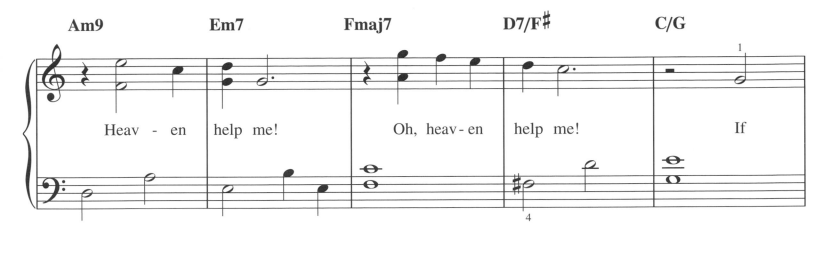

Am9   Em7   Fmaj7   D7/F♯   C/G

Heav - en help me! Oh, heav - en help me! If

F/G   G7sus   G/A

heav - en can't, _____ who can? Heav - en helps _

_ the man. Heav - en helps the man. Who can? Heav - en helps _

Am

_ the man. _____ I'm free!

LET'S MAKE BELIEVE WE'RE IN LOVE

Words by DEAN PITCHFORD
Music by TOM SNOW

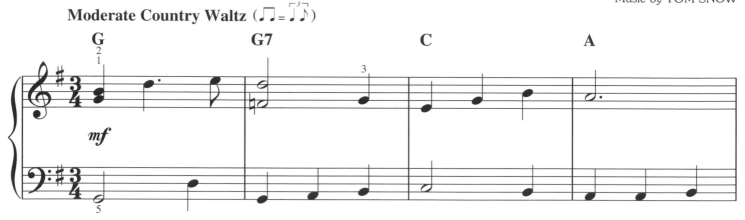

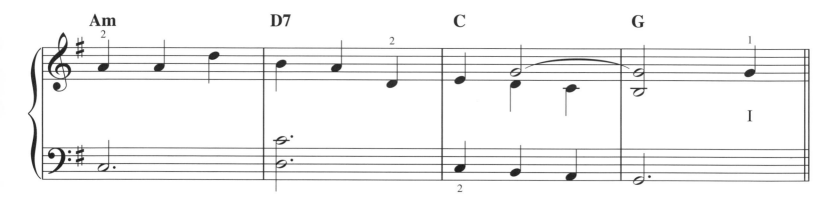

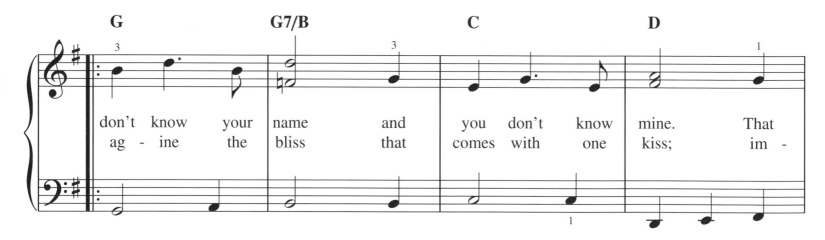

don't know your | name and | you don't know mine. | That
ag - ine the | bliss that | comes with one kiss; | im -

sounds like a | fine place to | start. | We are
ag - ine that | feel - ing won't | end. | There'll be

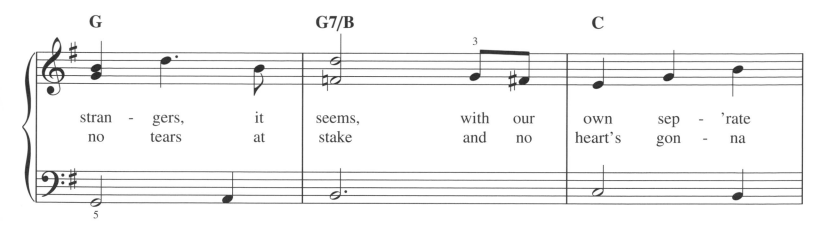

stran - gers, it seems, with our own sep - 'rate
no tears at stake and no heart's gon - na

dreams, but I feel like I know you by heart.}
break cuz it nev - er hurts to pre - tend.}

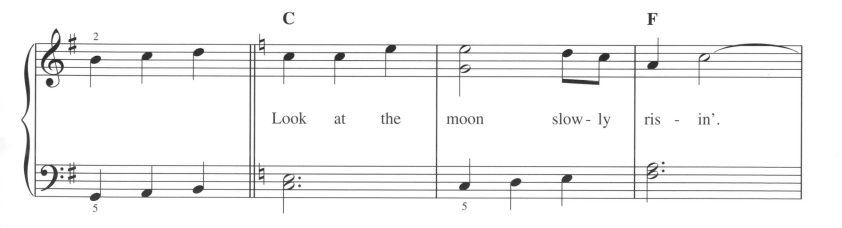

Look at the moon slow- ly ris - in'.

Look at those stars up a - bove.

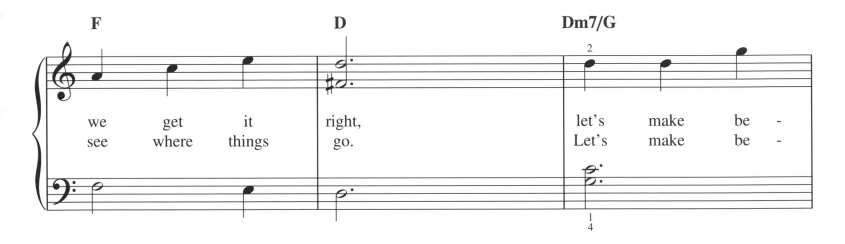

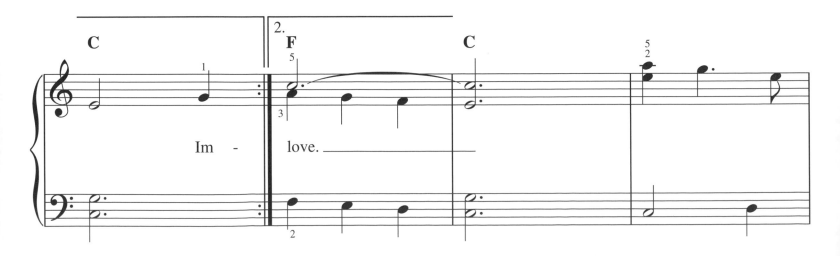

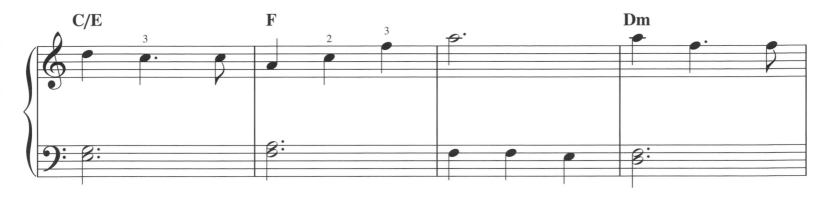

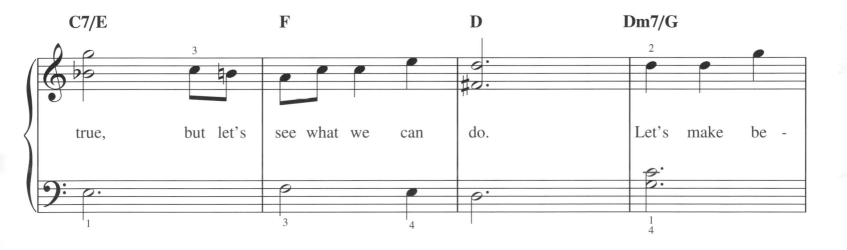

It may not yet be

true, but let's see what we can do. Let's make be -

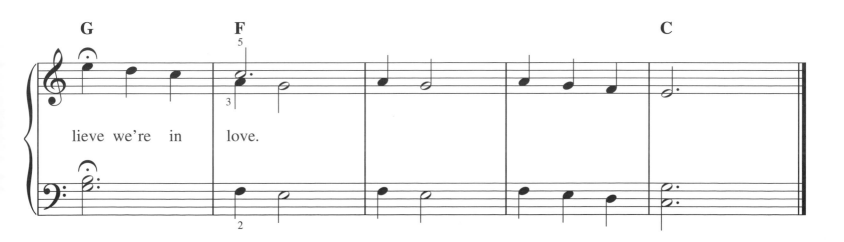

lieve we're in love.

LET'S HEAR IT FOR THE BOY

Words by DEAN PITCHFORD
Music by TOM SNOW

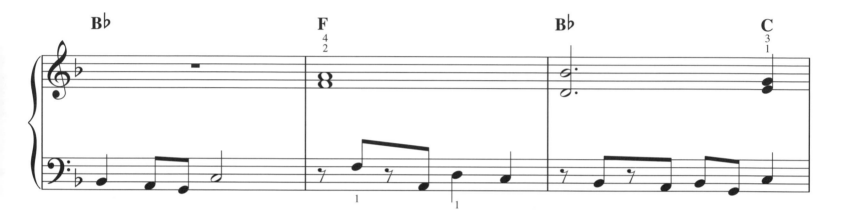

My | ba-by, he don't talk
ba-by may not be

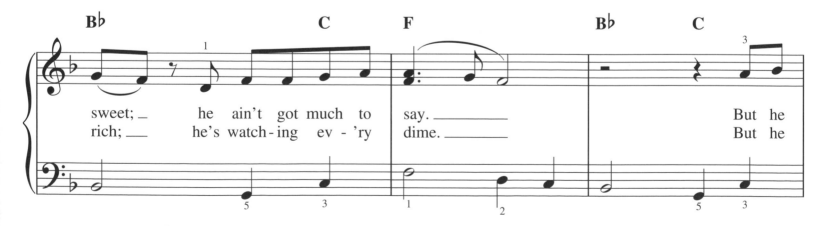

sweet; ___ he ain't got much to | say. ___ | But he
rich; ___ he's watch-ing ev-'ry | dime. ___ | But he

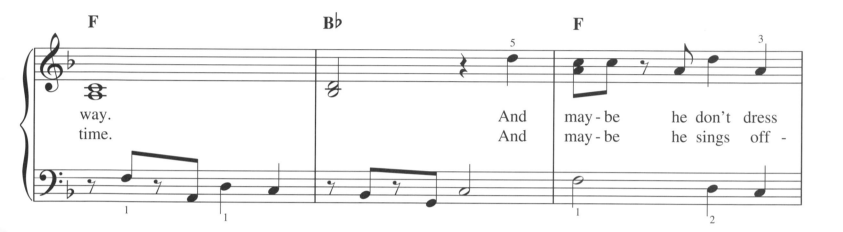

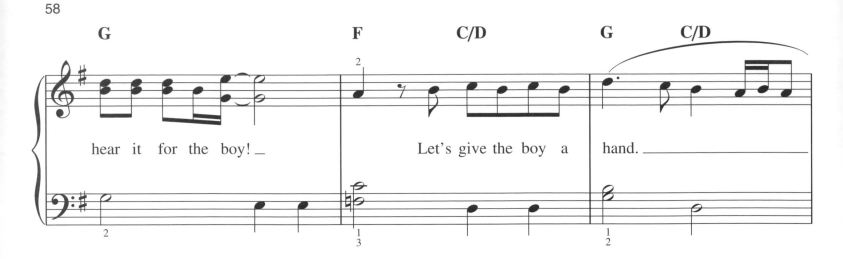

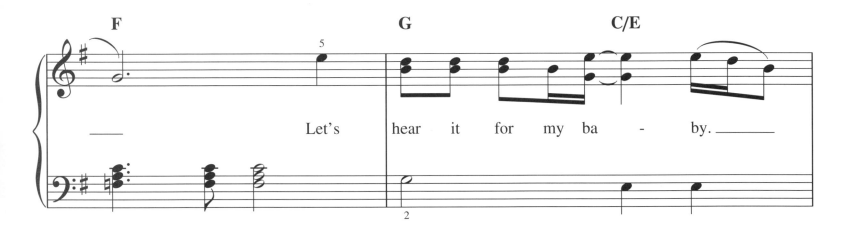

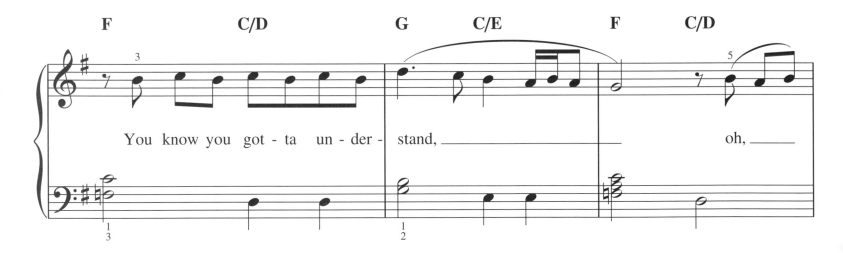

Whoa, whoa, whoa, whoa, let's hear it for the boy!

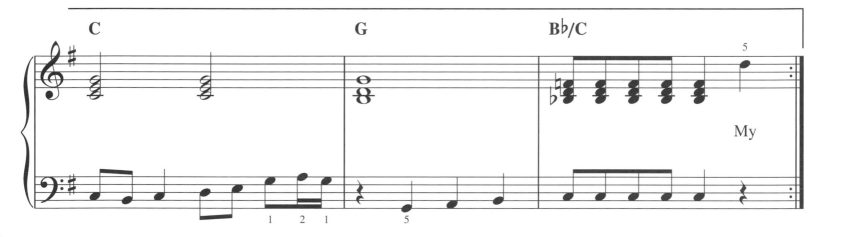

My

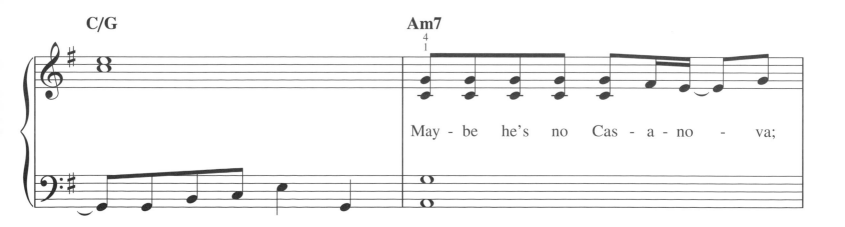

May - be he's no Cas - a - no - va;

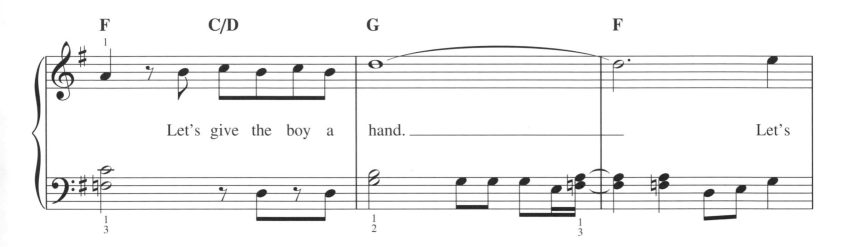

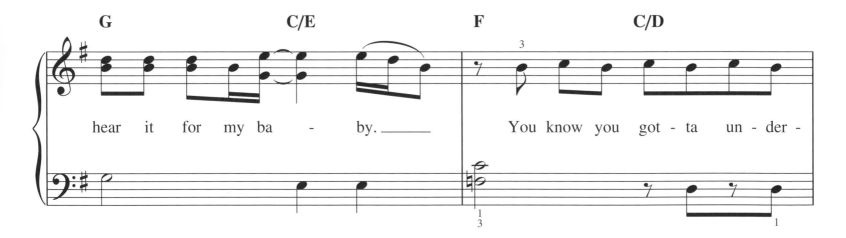

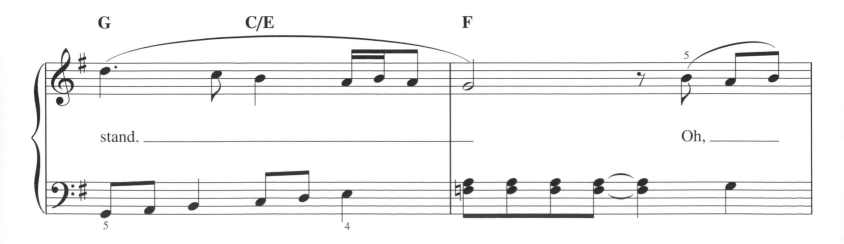

he don't score at Bowl - a - ra - ma; still, you got - ta thank his ma - ma.

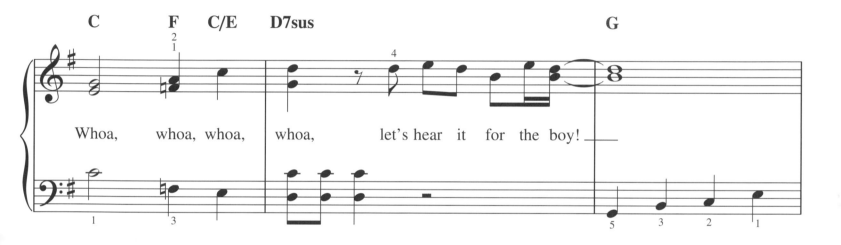

Whoa, whoa, whoa, whoa, let's hear it for the boy!

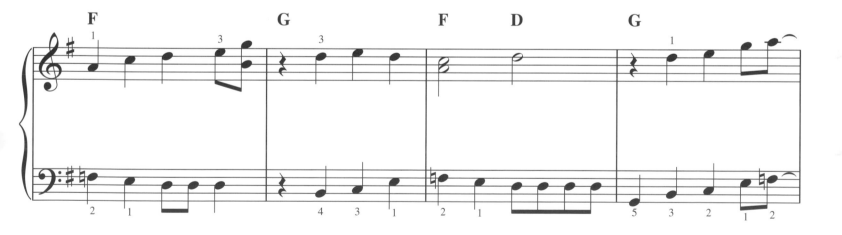

Let's hear it for my ba - by. ___ Hear it for the boy!

CAN YOU FIND IT IN YOUR HEART?

Words by DEAN PITCHFORD
Music by TOM SNOW

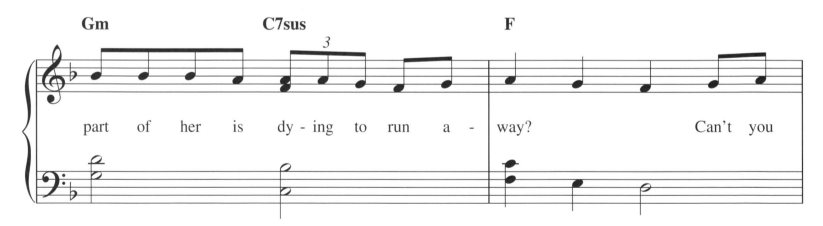

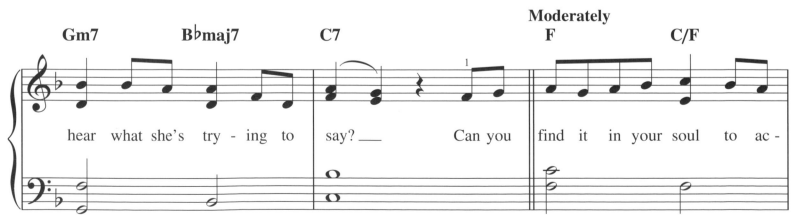

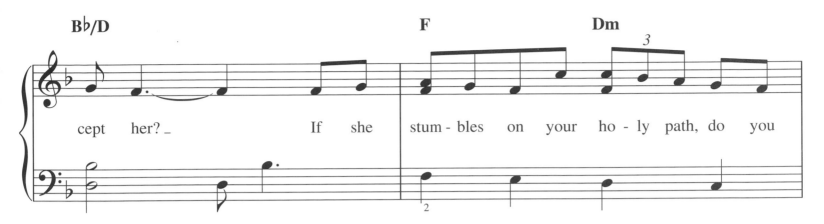

cept her? _ If she stum - bles on your ho - ly path, do you

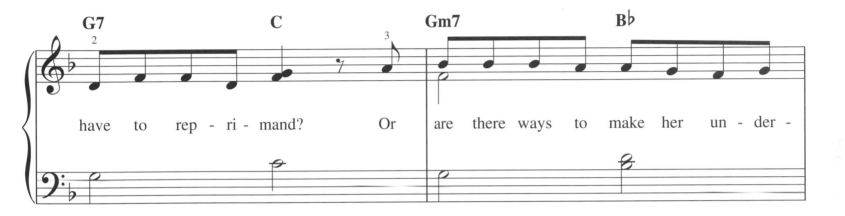

have to rep - ri - mand? Or are there ways to make her un - der -

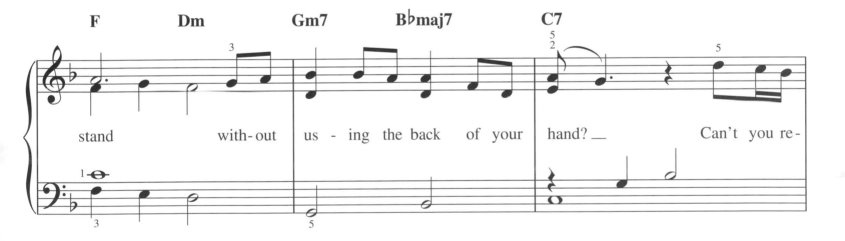

stand with-out us - ing the back of your hand? _ Can't you re-

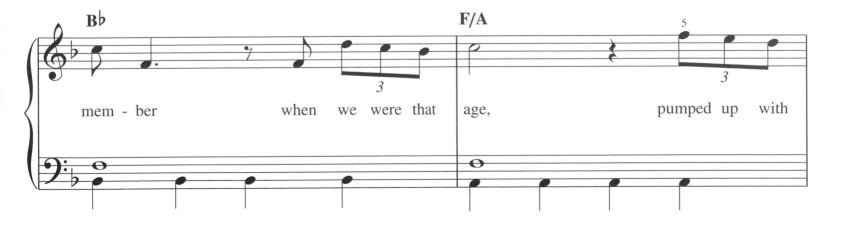

mem - ber when we were that age, pumped up with

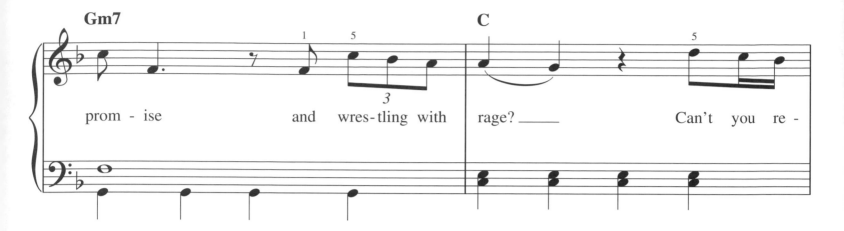

Gm7 .... **C**

prom - ise .... and wres-tling with .... rage? _____ .... Can't you re -

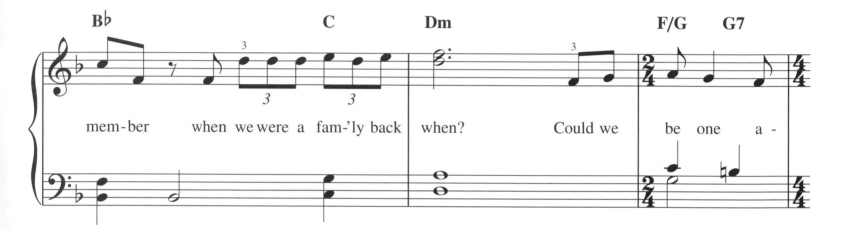

B♭ .... **C** .... **Dm** .... **F/G** **G7**

mem - ber .... when we were a fam-'ly back .... when? .... Could we .... be one a -

C9 .... **C** .... **G/B** **Am7**

gain?

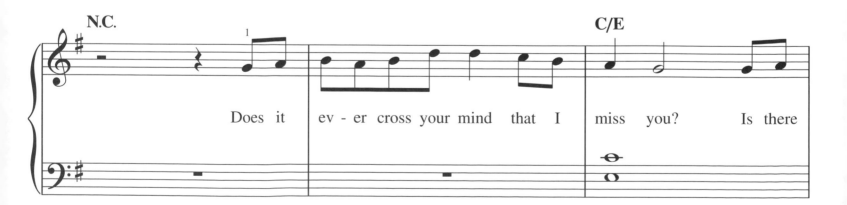

N.C. .... **C/E**

Does it .... ev - er cross your mind that I .... miss you? .... Is there

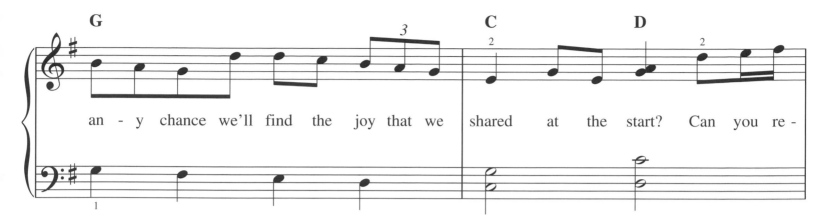

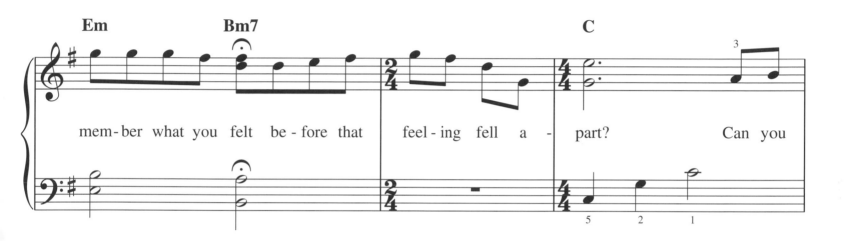

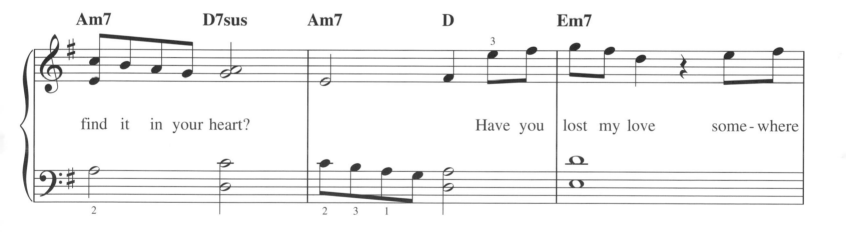

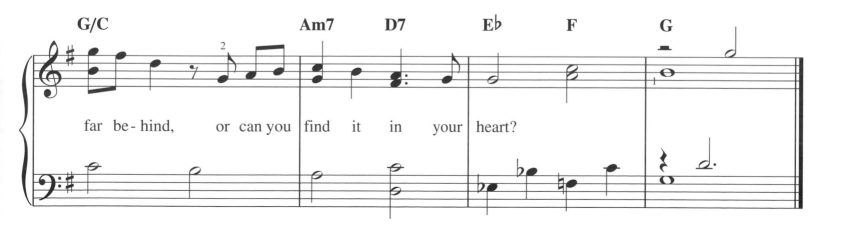

MAMA SAYS

Words by DEAN PITCHFORD
Music by TOM SNOW

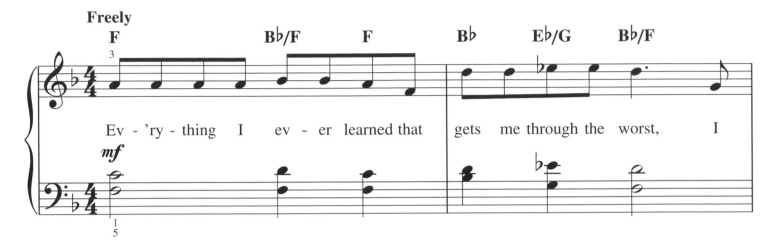

Ev - 'ry-thing I ev - er learned that gets me through the worst, I

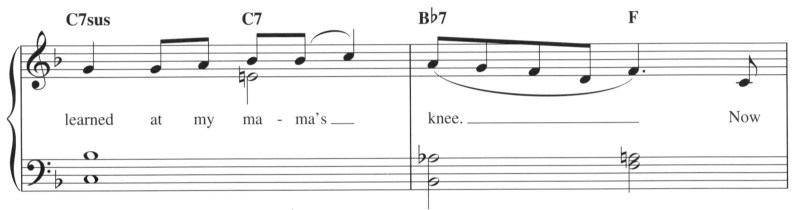

learned at my ma - ma's ___ knee. ___ Now

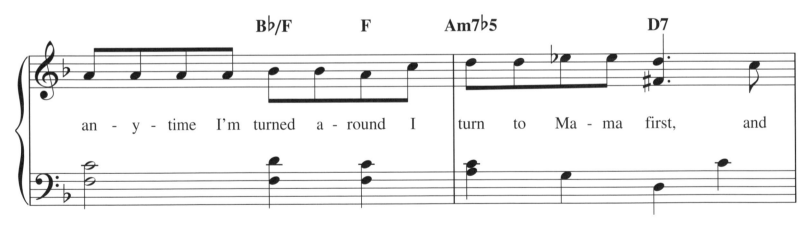

an - y-time I'm turned a - round I turn to Ma - ma first, and

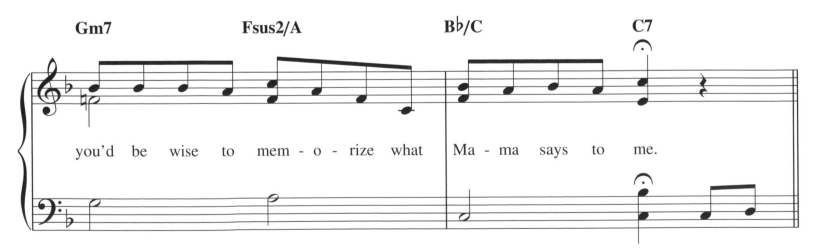

you'd be wise to mem - o - rize what Ma - ma says to me.

With a bayou beat

Spoken: Now, Mama ain't been wrong yet, and I'm living proof.

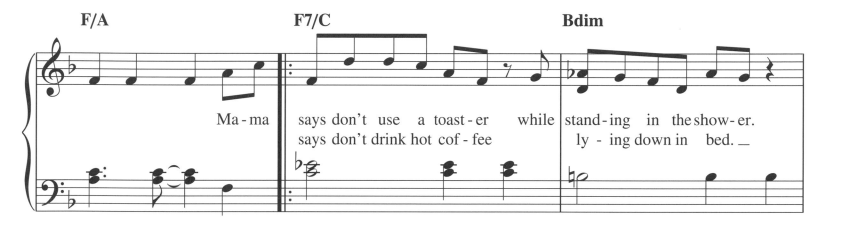

Ma - ma says don't use a toast - er while stand - ing in the show - er.
says don't drink hot cof - fee ly - ing down in bed. __

Now who can ar - gue with that? _____ Ma - ma
Don't e - ven give it a thought. __ Ma - ma

says don't hold your breath for long - er than an hour. __
says nev - er eat an - y - thing that's big - ger than your head. __

The wom - an knows where it's at!
Is she a whiz ___ or what?

And Ma - ma says

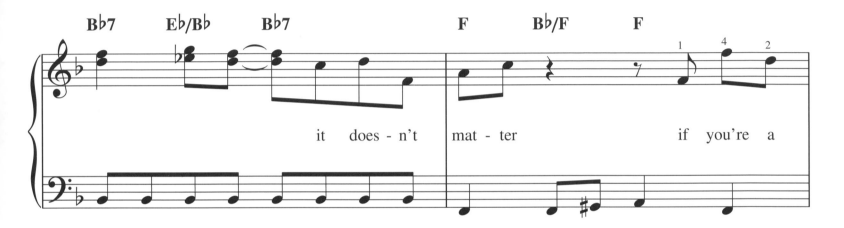

it does - n't mat - ter

if you're a

king

or you're a

clown.

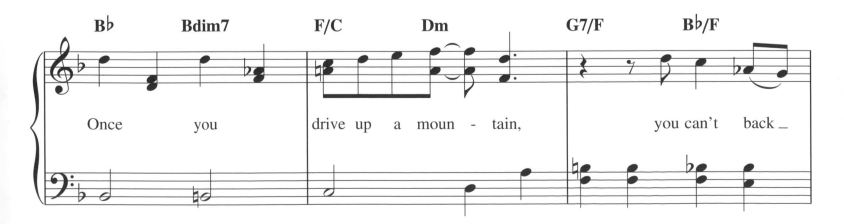

Once you

drive up a moun - tain,

you can't back ___

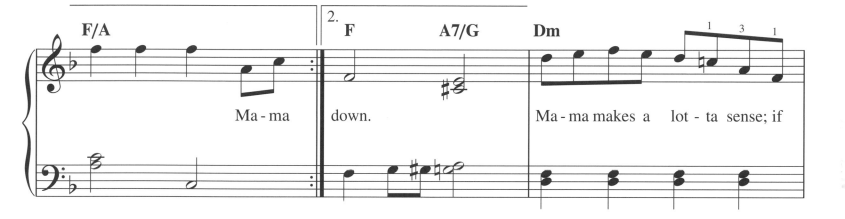

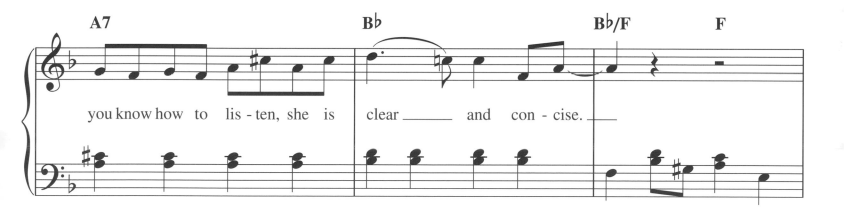

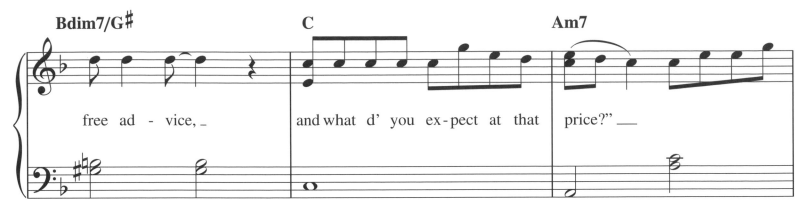

free ad - vice, _ and what d' you ex - pect at that price?" _

Ma - ma says what you be - lieve in ___ is

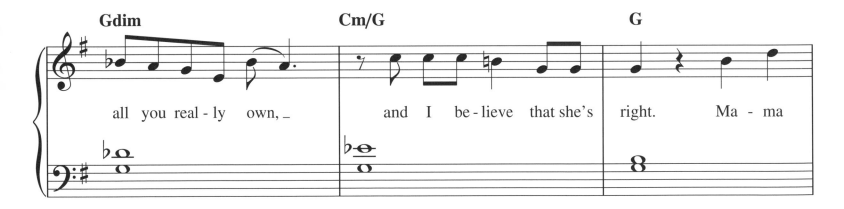

all you real - ly own, _ and I be - lieve that she's right. Ma - ma

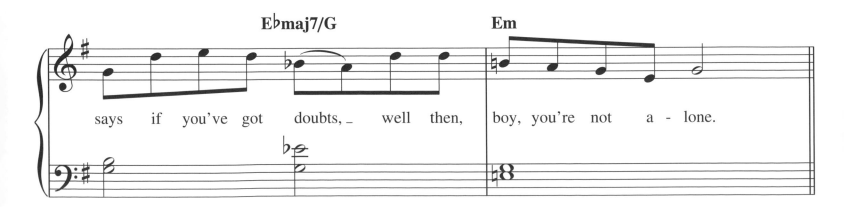

says if you've got doubts, _ well then, boy, you're not a - lone.

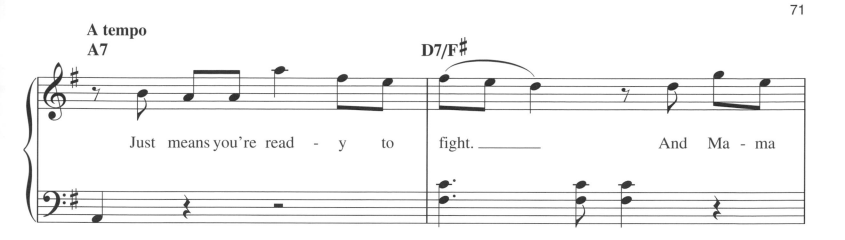

A tempo
A7 ... **D7/F#**

Just means you're read-y to fight._____ And Ma-ma

C ... **C/D** ... **G** ... **C** ... **C/D**

says _____ it does-n't mat-ter if you're a king _____ or you're a

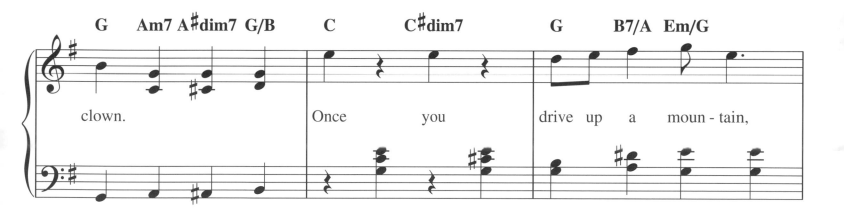

G **Am7** **A#dim7** **G/B** ... **C** ... **C#dim7** ... **G** **B7/A** **Em/G**

clown. Once you drive up a moun-tain,

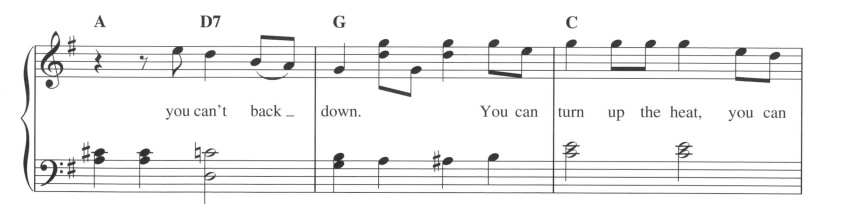

A ... **D7** ... **G** ... **C**

you can't back _ down. You can turn up the heat, you can

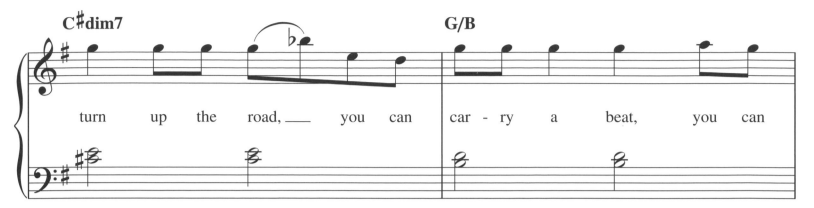

turn up the road, ___ you can | car - ry a beat, you can

car - ry a load, _ you can | throw a fit, you can | throw a punch, you can

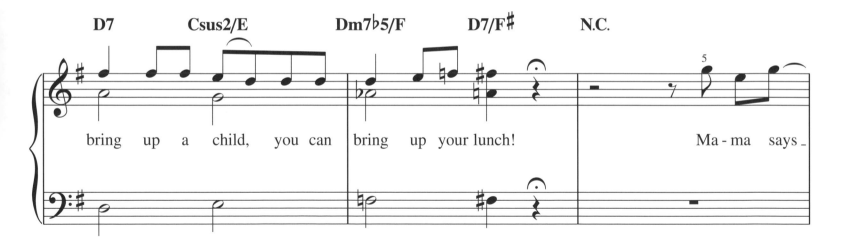

bring up a child, you can | bring up your lunch! | Ma - ma says _

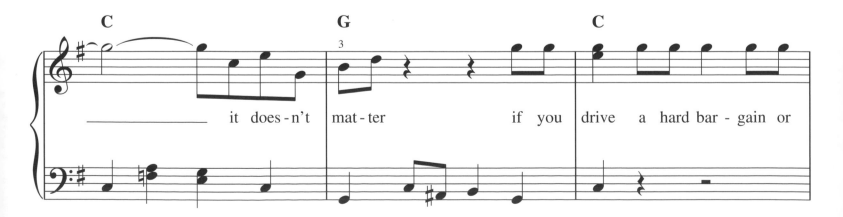

_____ it does - n't | mat - ter | if you drive a hard bar - gain or

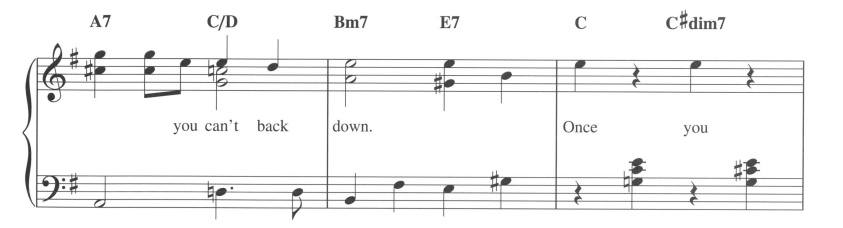

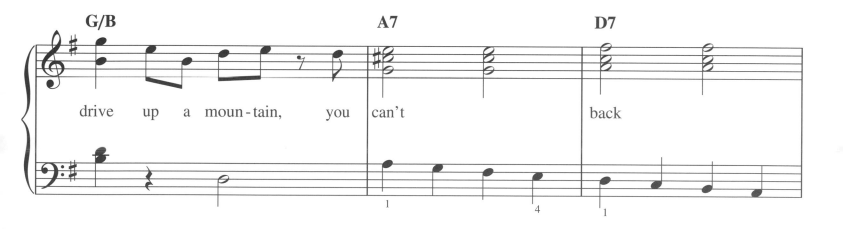

ALMOST PARADISE

Words by DEAN PITCHFORD
Music by ERIC CARMEN

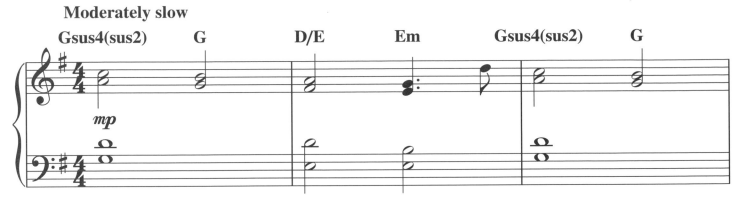

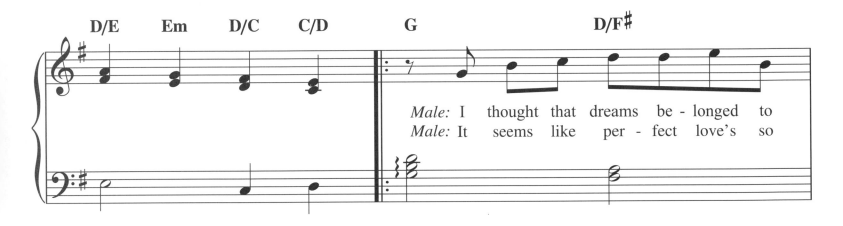

Male: I thought that dreams be-longed to
Male: It seems like per - fect love's so

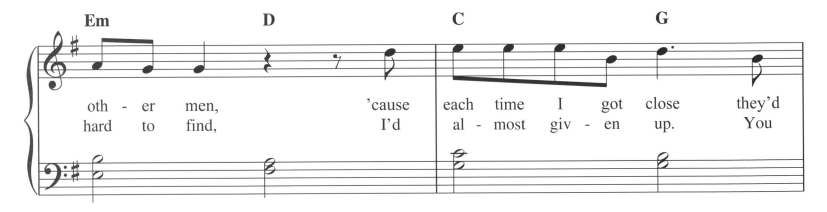

oth - er men, 'cause each time I got close they'd
hard to find, I'd al - most giv - en up. You

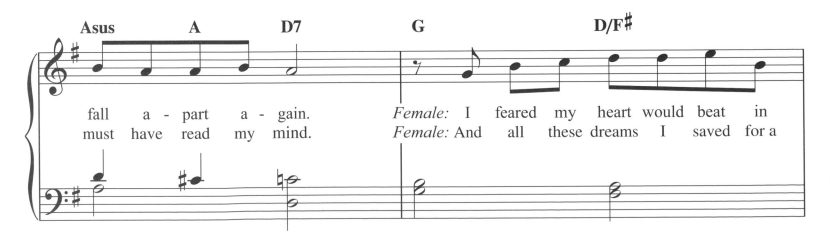

fall a - part a - gain. Female: I feared my heart would beat in
must have read my mind. Female: And all these dreams I saved for a

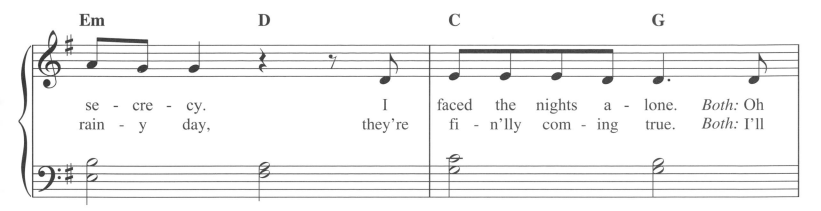

se - cre - cy.   I   faced the nights a - lone. *Both:* Oh
rain - y day,   they're fi - n'lly com - ing true. *Both:* I'll

how could I have known   that all my life I on - ly need - ed
share them all with you, 'cause now we hold the fu - ture in our

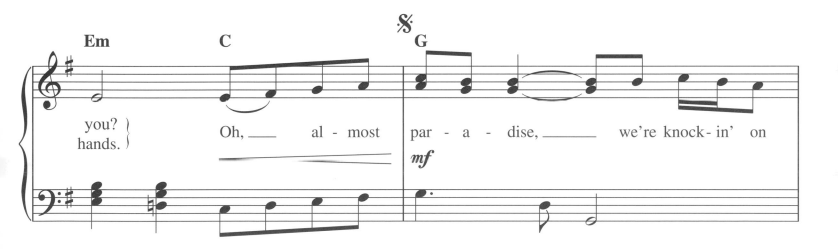

you? }
hands. }   Oh, ___ al - most par - a - dise, ___ we're knock - in' on

mf

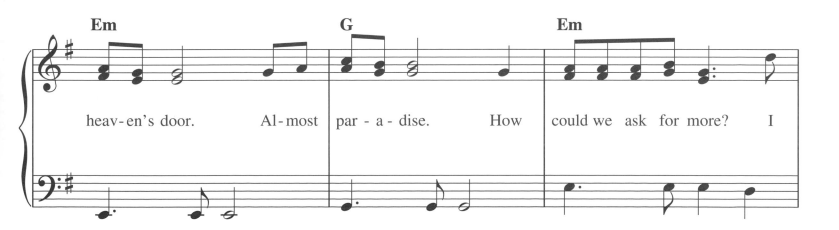

heav - en's door. Al - most par - a - dise. How could we ask for more? I

To Coda ⊕

swear that I can see for-ev-er in your __ eyes. | Par - a - dise.

1. D/E Em D/C C/D | **2.** C/G G E♭

Male:
And in your arms, sal - va-tion's

D.S. al Coda

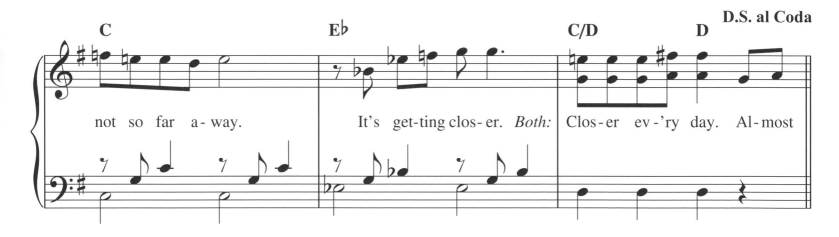

C E♭ C/D D

not so far a - way. | It's get-ting clos- er. *Both:* Clos- er ev -'ry day. Al-most

CODA ⊕ D/E Em D/C C/D C/G G G(add9)

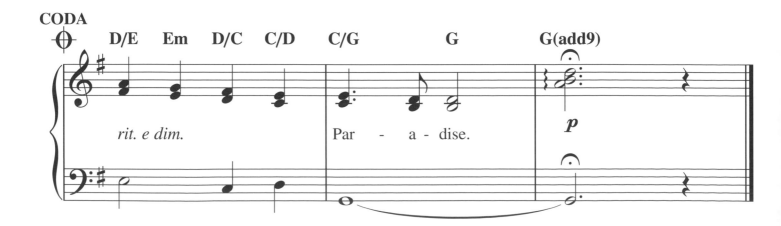

rit. e dim. | Par - a - dise. | *p*

I CONFESS

Words by DEAN PITCHFORD
Music by TOM SNOW

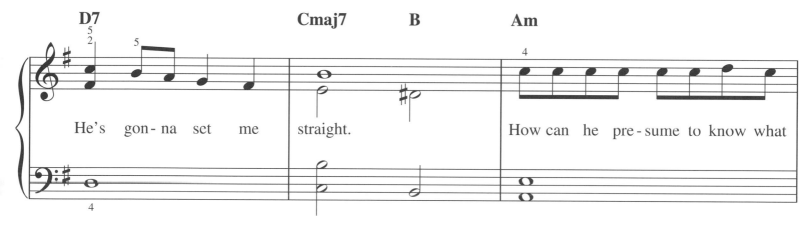

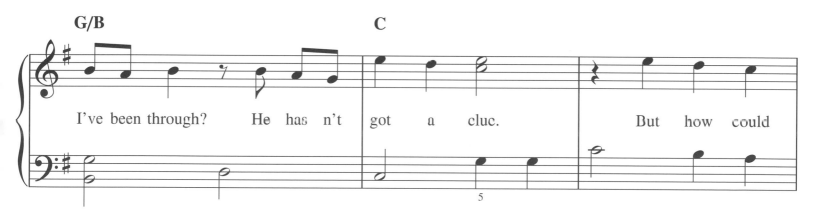

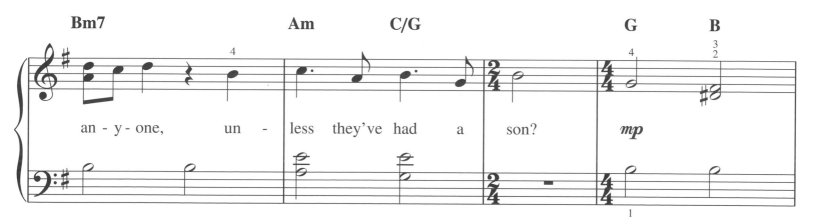

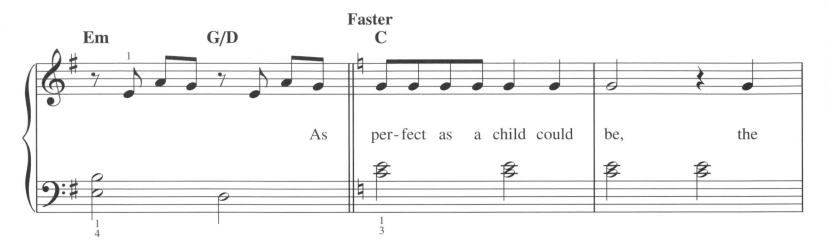

As per-fect as a child could be, the

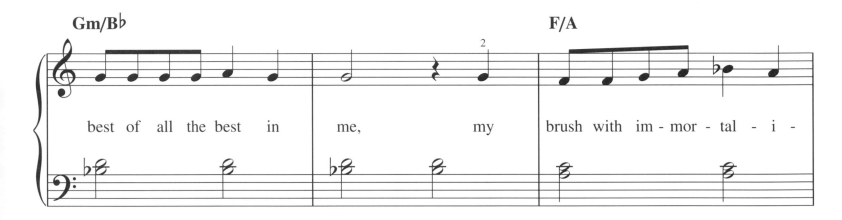

best of all the best in me, my brush with im - mor - tal - i -

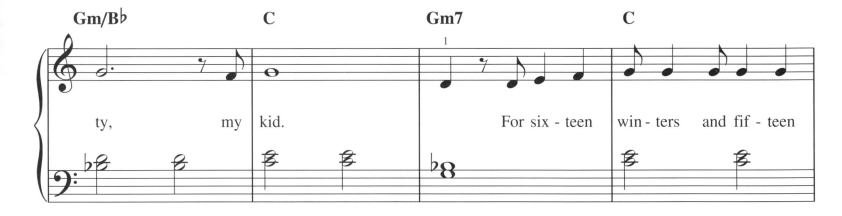

ty, my kid. For six - teen win - ters and fif - teen

springs, I had a son, and still it stings when I re - mem - ber

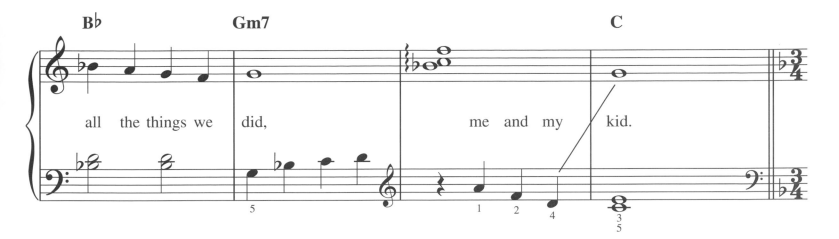

all the things we did, me and my kid.

Happily

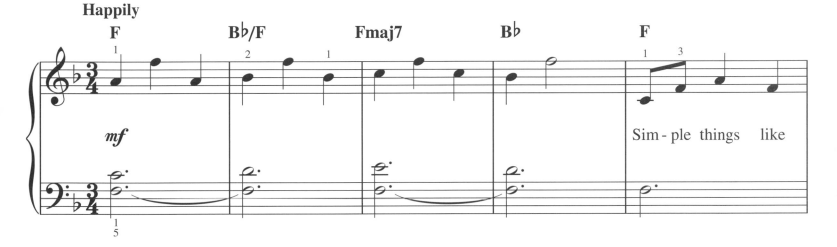

Sim - ple things like

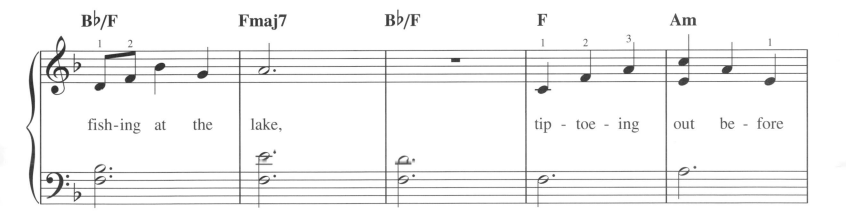

fish-ing at the lake, tip - toe - ing out be - fore

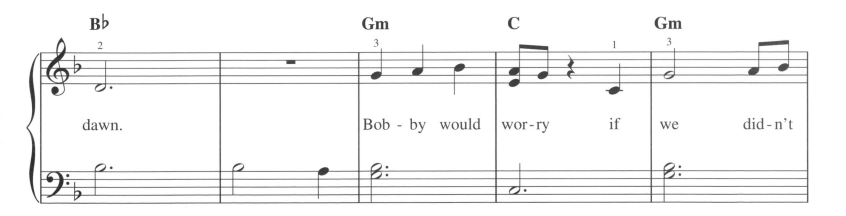

dawn. Bob - by would wor - ry if we did-n't

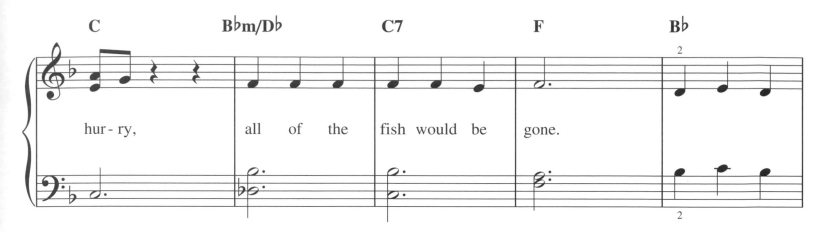

hur - ry, all of the fish would be gone.

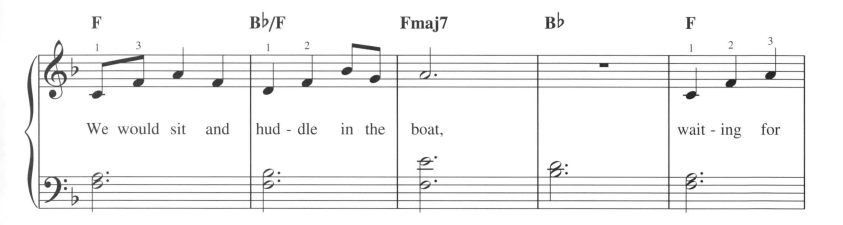

We would sit and hud - dle in the boat, wait - ing for

some - thing to bite, and I'd watch the sun - rise in my

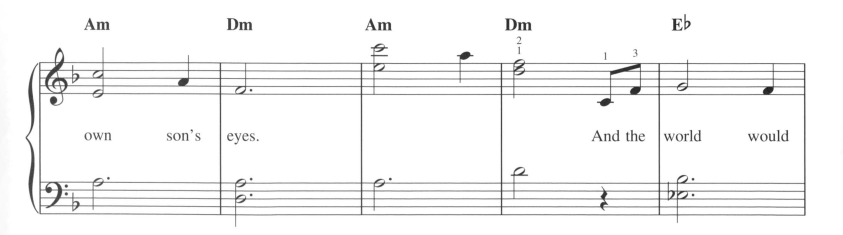

own son's eyes. And the world would

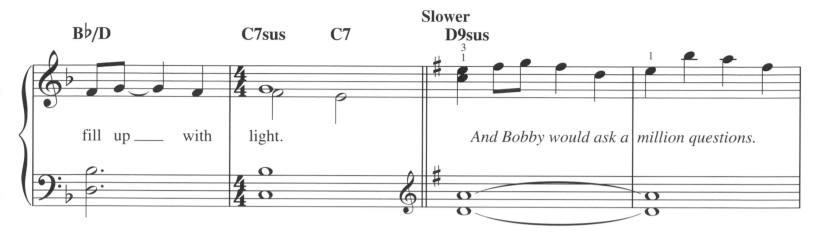

fill up ___ with | light. | *And Bobby would ask a* | *million questions.*

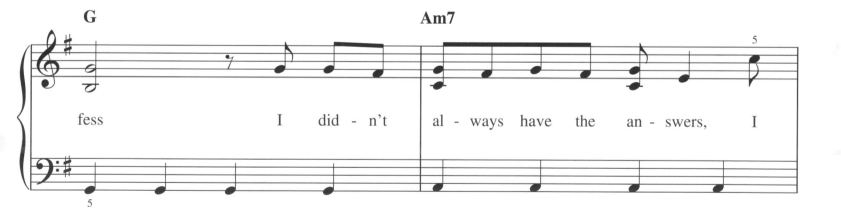

"Daddy, how many is the | *biggest number?"* Or | *"Daddy, why do I have a* | *thumb?"* And I con-

fess | I did - n't | al - ways have the an - swers, I

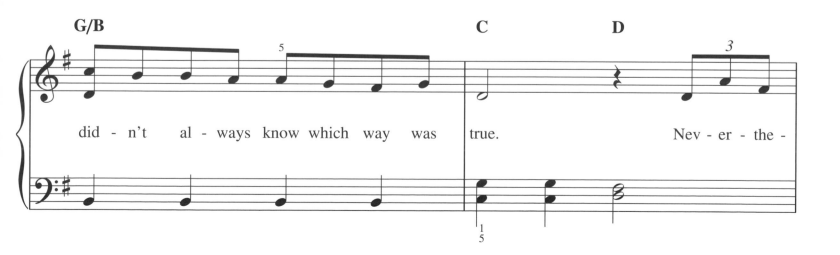

did - n't al - ways know which way was | true. | Nev - er - the-

82

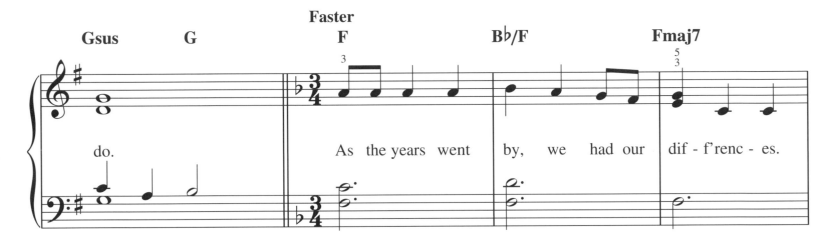

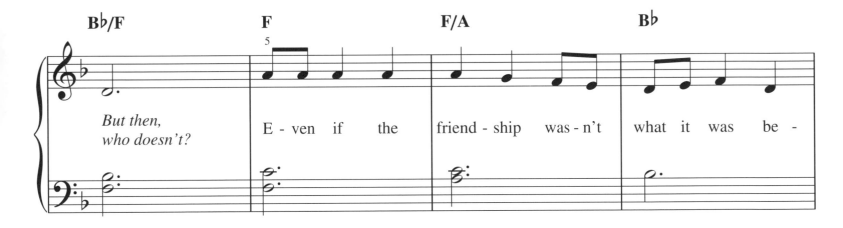

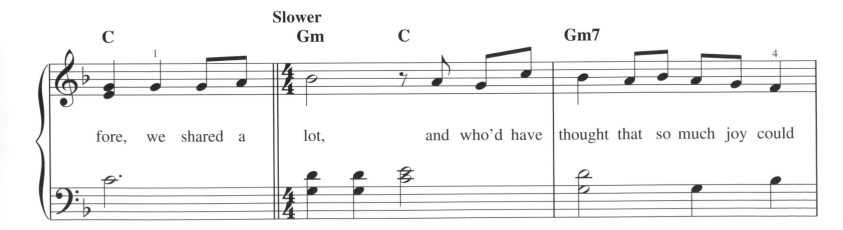

vanish in a blink? Who ever stops to think? And in that final moment

who knows what went wrong? The questions come too late and

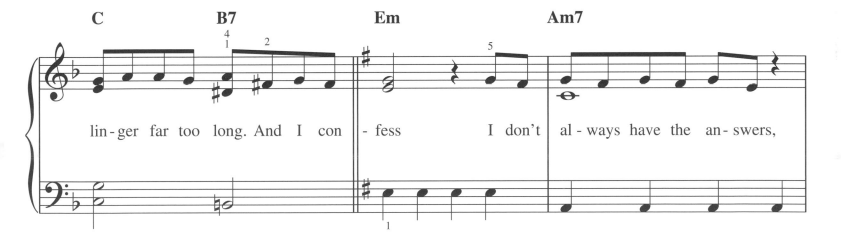

linger far too long. And I confess I don't always have the answers,

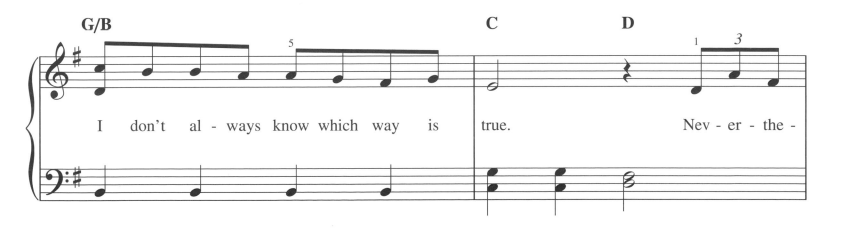

I don't always know which way is true. Neverthe-

less, I've al-ways tried to lead with love. That's all that an-y fa-ther can

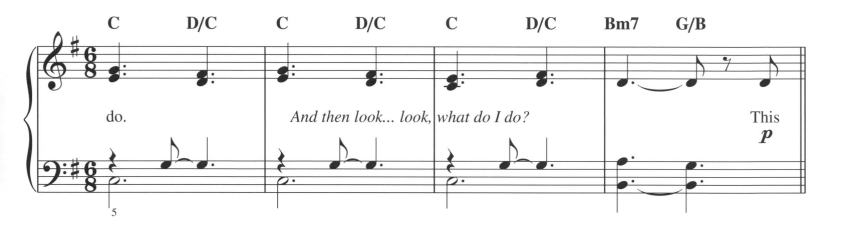

do. *And then look... look, what do I do?* This

p

With growing intensity

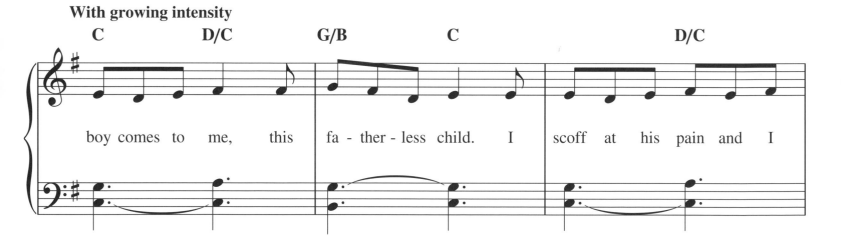

boy comes to me, this fa-ther-less child. I scoff at his pain and I

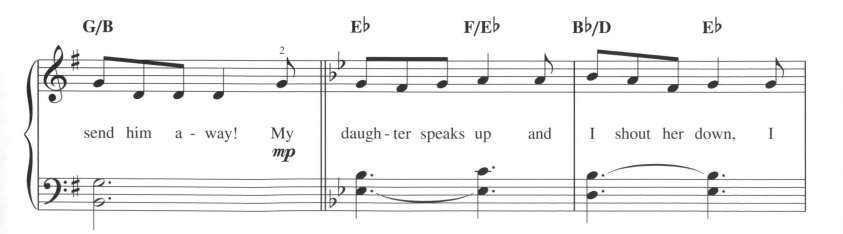

send him a-way! My daugh-ter speaks up and I shout her down, I

mp

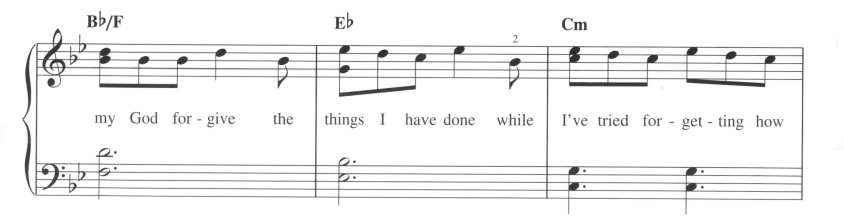

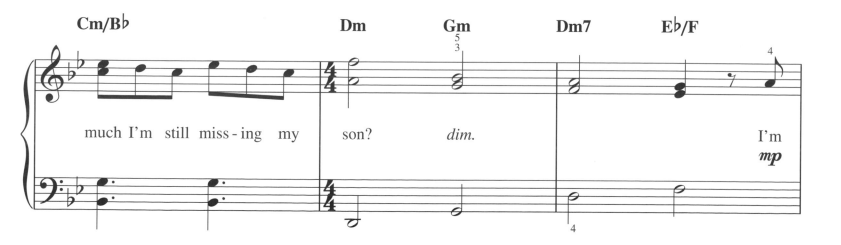

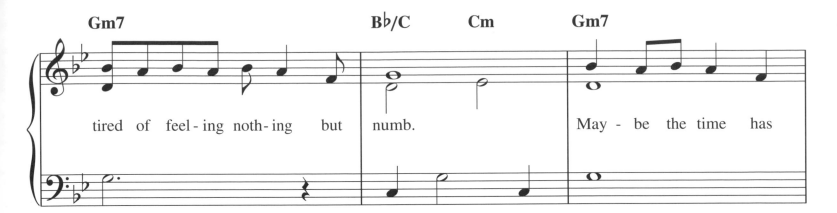

tired of feel-ing noth-ing but numb. May - be the time has

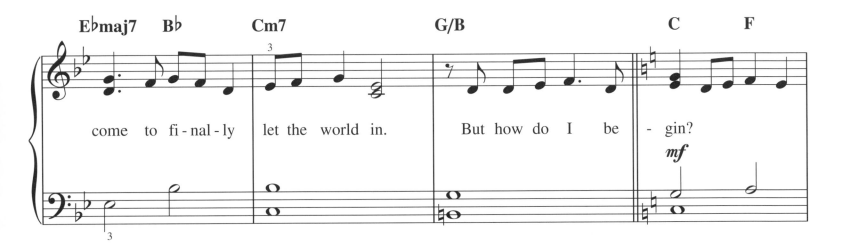

come to fi-nal-ly let the world in. But how do I be - gin?

mf

Give me strength and

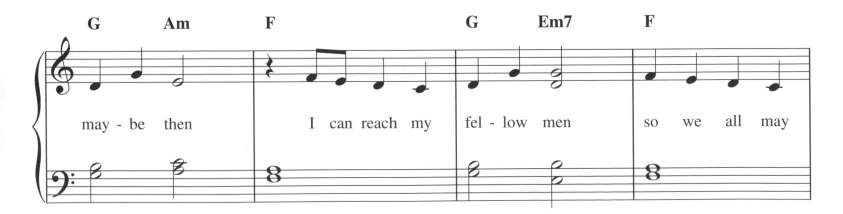

may - be then I can reach my fel - low men so we all may

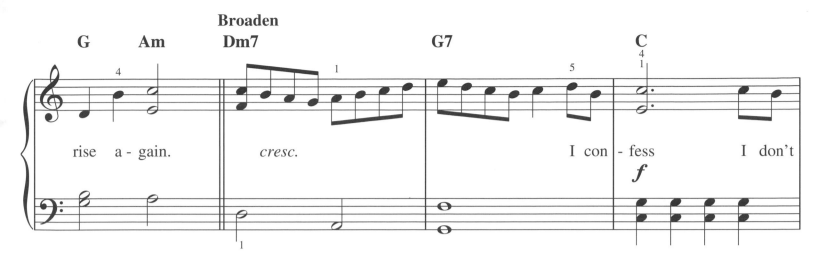

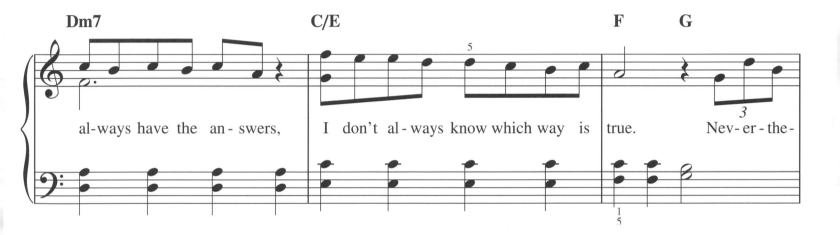

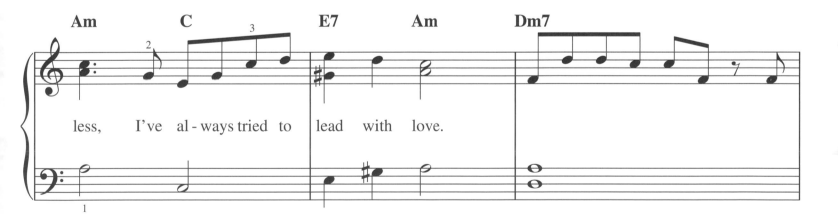

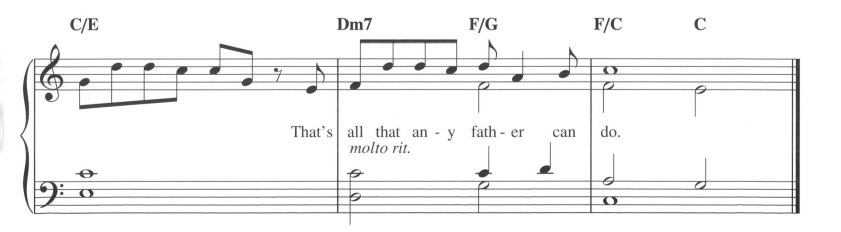